Heinzen Karl

The rights of women and the sexual relations

an address to an unknown lady reader

Heinzen Karl

The rights of women and the sexual relations
an address to an unknown lady reader

ISBN/EAN: 9783742815637

Manufactured in Europe, USA, Canada, Australia, Japa

Cover: Foto ©Thomas Meinert / pixelio.de

Manufactured and distributed by brebook publishing software
(www.brebook.com)

Heinzen Karl

The rights of women and the sexual relations

THE RIGHTS OF WOMEN

AND THE

SEXUAL RELATIONS

AN ADDRESS TO AN UNKNOWN LADY READER

BY

KARL HEINZEN

BOSTON, MASS.:
BENJ. R. TUCKER, PUBLISHER
1891

PREFACE.

THE following treatise comes from the pen of one of the most enlightened and humanitarian spirits of our time, whose libertarian and reformatory labors were not limited to his German fatherland and this republic, his adopted home, but extended to the entire civilized world by their unique and masterful many-sidedness. The author, who, after he had broken his fetters in despotic Europe, lived in this country during the larger and most fertile period of his life and brought to light his ripest spiritual treasures here, unfortunately remained unknown to the great majority of his American fellow-citizens. He counted as his friends only the most enlightened men of his time who could appreciate his quiet greatness. This remarkable fact, I believe, may be explained by the observations which the life-long friend of Karl Heinzen, Dr. Marie E. Zakrzewska of Boston,

iii

embodied in her autobiography,* dedicated to
the well-known American poetess, Mary L. Booth:
" The German mind, so much honored in Europe
for its scientific capacity, for its consistency regarding principles, and its correct criticism, is not
dead here; but it has to struggle against difficulties too numerous to be detailed here; and
therefore it is that the Americans don't know of
its existence, and the chief obstacle is their different languages. A Humboldt must remain unknown here, unless he chooses to Americanize
himself in every respect: and could he do this
without ceasing to be Humboldt, the cosmopoli-
tan genius?"

Among the friends of Heinzen referred to,
Wendell Phillips, William Lloyd Garrison, and
Charles Sumner are especially to be mentioned.
At the memorial gathering held on February 22,
1881 (Heinzen died November 12, 1880), Wendell
Phillips said concerning him:

---

* Practical Illustration of Woman's Right to Labor; or, A
Letter from Marie E. Zakrzewska, M.D. Edited by Caroline
H. Dall, author of " Historical Pictures Retouched," etc., etc.
Boston: Walker, Wise & Co. 1860. A book that ought to be
read by everybody who is interested in the solution of the
woman's question.

"I never met him on the streets without a feeling of the highest respect, and this respect I paid the rare, almost unexampled courage of the man. Mr. Heinzen in this respect stands almost alone among the immigrants to these shores. His idea of human right had no limitation. His respect for the rights of a human being as such was not to be shaken. The temptation to use his talent to gain reputation, money, power, at a time when, a poor emigrant, he lacked all these and was certain of acquiring them, was great; yet all these he laid calmly aside for the sake of the eternal principle of right, of freedom. He espoused the detested slave cause at a time when to do so meant poverty, desertion of fellow-countrymen, scorn, persecution even. Thus he acted in every cause. What seemed to him right, after the most unsparing search for truth, he upheld no matter at what cost. During the war, feeling that through ignorance or timidity on the part of Lincoln's government precious lives and treasures were being wasted, he was foremost among a few leading men who proposed the nomination of Fremont for the presidency. We had many private meetings and much correspondence with leading men in New York. I shall never forget 'some of these conversations with Mr. Heinzen. He was so far-seeing and sagacious ; he was so ingenious and contriving ; his judgment so penetrating.

"One other characteristic he had, belonging only to truly great men.   There was a kind of serenity and dignity about him, as one sure of the right in the course which he took, in the principles which he stated.   He was far in advance of other minds ; but he was sure in his trust in human nature that all others would come, must come to the same point with himself.   He could wait.   Few possessing equal mental ability are able also to do this.   The greatest courage is to dare to be wholly consistent.   This courage Heinzen showed when a little yielding, so little as would have been readily pardoned on the ground of common-sense, would have gained him popularity, fame, money, power.   He remained true to himself.

"Prominent men gained much from him, but never acknowledged their obligations.   He shaped many minds that led and created public opinion. His indeed was a life of trial, gladly borne without murmur of complaint, and his reward must be in the future.

"When I think of that lofty life there come

always to my mind those words of Tocqueville
which Sumner loved to quote: ' Remember life
is neither pain nor pleasure ; it is serious business, to be entered upon with courage, with the
spirit of self-sacrifice.' Surely if any life ever
exemplified that ideal, it is the one we meet to
remember and, as far as we can, to imitate—that
of Karl Heinzen."

As a German-American writer has said of him,
Heinzen was what Goethe called *eine Natur ;* that
is, a character of singularly original development,
a man of one mould, who remained true to himself in all conditions of life, and who valued this
fidelity to self higher than all external positions
and all the favors of the world. He knew of no
loftier ambition than obedience to his own teachings: "Learn to endure everything, only not
slavery; learn to dispense with everything, only
not with your self-respect ; learn to lose everything, only not yourself. All else in life is worth-
less, delusive, and fickle. Man's only sure support is in himself, in his individuality, resting in
its own power and sovereignty." Besides he was
a writer who knew how to wield his pen as almost
none of his contemporaries, certainly not one of
the writers of the German tongue in this coun-

try ; who as none else knew how to express his thoughts in the most pregnant, incisive, and energetic form—a master of pure classical style.

That a spirit who could proclaim such principles was bound to throw his entire revolutionary energy on the side of the liberation of woman from the fetters of social and political slavery is a matter of course.

The treatise here submitted, which appeared for the first time in the German language in 1852 and later in an expanded form in 1875, is translated into English by an American lady of German descent, Mrs. Emma Heller Schumm, of Boston ;*

---

* Perhaps this is the proper place to state that, greatly as I admire and esteem the character and genius of Karl Heinzen, I cannot entirely agree with all the views laid down in the following treatise. From some of the positions taken therein I emphatically dissent. Not where he is most radical and thoroughgoing in his advocacy of liberty in the sexual relations and of the independence of woman, for I am with him there ; but where he seems to forget his radicalism, and to lose his grand confidence in the power of liberty to rejuvenate, to regulate, and to moderate, and falls back upon the State for that readjustment and guidance of human affairs which one day will be accomplished only in liberty and by liberty,—it is there where I radically dissent; and I make this statement for the sake of setting myself right with those who happen to be acquainted with my views on these points.

Goethe says somewhere: "*Die Menschen werden durch Meinungen getrennt, durch Gesinnungen vereinigt*"—Men are and it is the intention of the publisher, in case the demand for this treatise should give him any encouragement, to continue the publication in English translation of the immortal treasures of

---

separated by their opinions, but united by the spirit that governs them. Thus, notwithstanding our disagreement as regards the manner of attaining a desirable end, I am proud to call myself a follower of Karl Heinzen as regards the spirit with which he approached all questions of human concern. This spirit, as well as the fundamental ideas underlying the following treatise, cannot, as I take it, be better epitomized than by the following quotation from the pen of one of the contributors to "Liberty" of Boston :

"Woman's emancipation means freedom, liberty. It means liberty pure and simple; failing of which, it is, according to its degree, oppression, suppression, tyranny. It means liberty to enter any and all fields of labor,—trade, profession, science, literature, and art,—and liberty to compete for the highest positions in the land. Liberty to choose her companion, and equal liberty to change. Liberty to embrace motherhood in her own way, time, and place, and freedom from the unjustly critical verdict and action of society concerning her movements. She will no longer recognize society's right to condemn in *her* practices condoned in man. No more a slave, she will be a true comrade; independent of man, as he is independent of her; dependent on him, as he is dependent on her. And the sex question will be settled. All this, and more, when woman shall be free, and enjoy an equality of liberty with man."

And in this view my task in getting out the treatise now for the first time submitted to the English-reading-public has been a source of great delight to me, and I can only join with Mr. Schmemann in the hope that women will give it the welcome it deserves, and that it may point out the way to liberty to many an oppressed sister.—TRANSLATOR.

Heinzen's thought and thus make them accessible to the American reading public.

In this treatise the cause of the emancipation of woman finds its most brilliant championship, as it has hardly ever before been discussed with less reserve and greater freedom. I cherish the hope that its circulation will largely contribute towards enlightening the public on this most important question, in order thereby to hasten its speedy solution. The translator as well as the publisher would in that case feel themselves amply rewarded for their unselfish labor, while the lofty intentions of the author would meet with their full realization.

KARL SCHMEMANN.

DETROIT, June, 1891.

THE RIGHTS OF WOMEN AND THE SEXUAL RELATIONS.

AN ADDRESS TO AN UNKNOWN LADY READER.

Notwithstanding all reactionary precautions, there is a spirit of liberty breathing through the world that lifts the veil from all lies and the roofs from all dungeons in order to show mankind how much truth it has failed to grasp, and how much justice it has crushed. It is a sad task to accompany this spirit on its flight and to note the countless aberrations of mankind; but it is an imperative duty to report what has been observed, and to participate in the reformation of this degenerate world.

Not only from the dungeons of famous martyred men, also from the chambers of nameless martyred women time has removed the covering roof. More than one-half of your sex consists of martyrs, aye, the history of your sex is one continuous story of martyrs. And while the oppressed of the stronger sex can read their sufferings in the fugitive history of states and nations, the sufferings of women find a place only in the long history of mankind.

This is beginning to be recognized, and among women themselves champions have at last arisen who demand that the age of slavery and suffering shall give place to an age of liberty and rights. Especially in America, the new Amazons who seek to humanize men, as those of history sought to slay them, form a very respectable phalanx.

And here, too, it is where a suitable battle-field is open to them, and where it is also possible to unite this battle-field with the arena of men. Especially in America, where so many questions are already solved which in Europe still call for the exertion of all forces, it is the part of men to occupy themselves with the important question of woman's emancipation; here more than else-where men of truly democratic spirit ought to make it their task to bring the discussion on this interesting and much-derided theme to a conclusion. It is a glaring anomaly to rejoice over the emancipation of the slaves and to treat the emancipation of woman with ridicule.

I venture the attempt of contributing my mite to the proposed work. In so doing I shall strive to be as clear, as radical, as brief, as just, but also as frank, as possible. In any case, dear reader, I am convinced that I have some new points of view to offer which deserve your attention.

But whoever you may be, in giving your attention to these pages may you be prevailed upon to publicly express your opinion on a common and important matter! But frankly, truthfully, and without reserve, as will be done here. False modesty is not only a weakness; it is also a fault, because it throws a suspicion on what it attempts to conceal. So long as we still shrink from speaking about human matters in a human manner we have not yet developed into true men and women; so long as we still play the hypocrite out of sheer "morality" we have not yet a conception of true morality; so long as we still seek for culture in the perversion of human nature we have no reason to boast of our culture. But in regard to the question of rights now under consideration, a radical straightforward examination of the relations of the two sexes to each other is an essential requisite for its solution.

There are three rocks upon which the truthfulness of the world, especially of the masculine world, is wont to come to grief and to change into the most intolerable and contemptible hypocrisy: the Revolution, Religion, and Love. Thousands want the revolution and feign legality; thousands are without religion and go to church; thousands seek the clandestine satisfaction of their sexual desires, while outwardly they mani-

fest the most studied indifference towards the
feminine sex. You will not have to accuse the
author of these pages of hypocrisy. He has given
complete expression to his opinions regarding the
revolution; he has done so regarding religion;
and he is now doing so regarding the two sexes.
Give him your support by reciprocating his frank-
ness, help him to examine the nature and the
needs of both sexes, in order thereby to establish
the claims which your sex has to make. You will
share with me the satisfaction that he who speaks
his convictions openly and completely before all
the world, and in spite of all the world, not only
acts more nobly, but also more successfully, than
all the reserve of prudence and all the hypocrisy
of cowardice are able to act.

The object to be gained here is not only to
purify humanity and the sense of justice from the
dross of a false morality and vulgar prejudice; nor
is our task limited to the rescue of love and marriage, which are in danger of perishing entirely in
this venal and pious world; it is at the same time
also necessary to open up to your sex a perspec-
tive view of the position which the era of liberty,
towards which our development is tending, will
assign to it in society. It will be seen that the
right, the happiness, and the lot of woman is still
more dependent on the attainment of complete
liberty than that of man, who at least finds a
partial compensation for liberty in the struggle

for it, and that the relation of the two sexes to each other can reach its true form only at the summit of political development from which we are still far enough removed, even in North America.

HISTORICAL REVIEW OF THE LEGAL
POSITION OF WOMEN.

As a rule history considers women only in so far as they occasionally exert an apparent influence upon the history of men.   The feminine half of humanity is usually overlooked like a superfluous appendage.   The women are weak, they are silent, they patiently suffer, they do not rebel, and that is sufficient to expose them to disregard, to make them historically irresponsible.   It would be of great interest to write a history from a radical point of view of the position which women have occupied among the different nations and in different ages in a social, political, and literary respect.   I would undertake to do this work if I were sufficiently well read, and if the necessary material were not wanting to me as well as the leisure to make exhaustive use of the latter.   I shall therefore content myself with giving from scant notes and recollections a brief survey, in order at least to uphold the leading idea that the position of women, dependent upon the general state of civilization and liberty of a people, can become an entirely just and honorable one only in that distant future in which the subordination of the right of brutal strength to the right of humane thought will have become a reality.

In the historical retrospect, in which we cannot always proceed chronologically, but merely according to the stages of civilization of various nations, we begin with the savage. It will be immaterial for the purpose whether we take examples of the Africa of to-day, or whether we trace the oldest nations of history back to their savage state. Savages are very much alike everywhere, and that all nations have at one time been in the savage state even those do not doubt who believe that man has been placed ready made into the world by a "God," the sum of all wisdom and civilization. To the savage physical strength is synonymous with right, and since the man has by nature more physical strength and aggressive passion than woman, the submission of the latter to the former is self evident. (Among animals nature seems to have equalized this relation somewhat, as the females of some species are larger than the males.) The savage associates the woman with himself because his sexual needs require her, and he controls her because he is the stronger. This control is carried to such an extent that the body of the woman is actually treated as a piece of furniture, and in some places is even guarded against foreign touch by some barbaric tailoring. With most savages the woman, besides being a concubine, is at the same time the slave and beast of burden of the man. Polygamy is likewise in accordance with this state of barbarity; polyandry,* on the other hand, is found rarely,—rather as a consequence of the presumption of the stronger, adultery is almost everywhere treated as a crime only on the part of women, while masculine adultery does not exist at all. But in spite of polygamy a selection is to be observed even among savages, a distinction of and temporary union with a single person. Rousseau, it is true, disputes this by maintaining that among savages every woman had the same value; it can be shown, however, by facts as well as by *à priori* demonstration that even the rudest savage has an eye and discrimination for superiority and qualities suitable to him in this or that woman, and feels the need of uniting himself more closely with the one he prefers. The analogy of animals also points that way, as there is among many animals an entirely exclusive conjugal relation at least during the breeding period. Why special stress is laid on these facts will become clear in the discussion of marriage.

The savage state is followed by the semi-civilized period, in which man settles down and forms a family life, and in accordance with it the woman

---

* It is said to have existed for a time among the ancient Medes, and at the present day is to be found only on the coast of Malabar and at the Himalayas, where it is kept up chiefly on account of the difficulty of supporting children.

plays the part of a member of the family, but of course without any independence whatever. On the contrary, in spite of her position in the family, she is deprived of all liberty, confined in a harem, and jealously watched. She exchanges open slavery for secret slavery; she remains now as before the tool of the man, only according to more definite rules and laws of external etiquette. In the harem the preference of individuals, already apparent among savages, becomes more strongly marked, although here also it does not lead to a real monogamic union. This state of things is, however, specifically oriental. But the degradation of women in the orient was so manifold that their social position cannot be designated by one word. With the Babylonians the marriageable maidens were taken to he market, examined by the men like any other ware, and bid for. It was also customary in the temple of Mylitta that every woman must extend her favors to strangers for money, which went into the pockets of the priests. Zoroaster abolished polygamy among the Persians after the institution of the harem had reached its highest development. It is well known that polygamy and traffic with women existed also among the Jews. The Mosaic price for a pretty woman was about five dollars. If the man wished to get rid of the woman he threw her out of the house.

In the next stage we find the woman as independent housewife, with more liberty of action, and more highly respected. The Homeric descriptions show this stage in its best light. The woman is no longer under surveillance, as in the harem, where the man visits her when it suits his pleasure and fancy, but she has also free access to the man. She has control of the department of the interior, is the hostess of the house, and does the honors in receiving guests. But in spite of this more favored position, the rights which are granted woman are rooted in the interests. and the will of the man, not in a true ethical recognition. The dependence of women was, on the contrary, still so great in this stage that the sons had the power to remarry their mothers to whomsoever they pleased; men could keep concubines as they liked, etc.

A further development marks the transition of private control of woman to public or political control of her. In this respect the Spartans took the lead with a truly classical despotism. With them every regard for nature, for humanity, for morality, for liberty disappeared before the regard for that State which Lycurgus seems to have called to life in order to show that mankind could furnish an energetic mind with the material for the realization of every extravagance. Women served the Spartans only for the bearing of children, of young Spartans. If children could be brought into the world by a mill or some other kind of machine, the Spartans would have abolished women, and introduced in their place State child factories. According to the purely political or patriotic purpose, which called for merely warlike manhood and coarse republican insensibility, the women received a thoroughly masculine training, and in order to guard them against the danger of effeminating the men and of occupying them too much by their charms, they were trained after their marriage for the manufacture of wool, and treated like factory implements. Woman, as such, did not exist in Sparta ; her femininity was rather a fault, and this fault was corrected through barbarity. Marriage proper was unknown to the Spartans. The men could visit the women only for a few minutes ; the object was merely to beget children. Weak or old men, by virtue of their right of control over their wives, brought them good breeders, and if any one was especially pleased with a woman he would ask, not her, but her husband, for the permission to beget a "noble child" with her—all this was done for State purposes, which had crowded out every other consideration, and would not allow the question of the existence of an independent inclination on the part of woman to be raised at all.

The Spartans furnish the classic example of that error which sacrifices to the enthusiasm for a political end, the end of all political endeavor, namely humanity, because they neglected to take

human nature into their council.   As long as the
world stands women have been the victims of this
error on the one side, and of Sultanic brutality on
the other, and it is doubtful whether they have
more reason to complain of the Sultans or of the
Spartans.

The treatment of women took on a milder and
more humane form with the more civilized and
more æsthetical Athenians.   But a real appreciation of woman was unknown even among that
people who adored the ideal of the fair sex in the
goddess of love, who had the most humane conception of love among all the nations, whose
mythology developed into the most beautiful and
most attractive romances of love, and who often
depicted in their poetry the feminine excellences
with the clearest perception.   Also among the
Athenians the State was in a certain sense the
despot; the State which received especial weight
by contrast with foreign foes, was the worldly
deity to which everything was sacrificed except
its priests, and these priests were, of course, the
men, the women were the victims.   The Athenians
also regarded the State as an end, not as means to
an end; they made it an object of religion rather
than the mere framework of the body social.
This State, this republic, was moreover continually called into question, now by native, now by
foreign tyrants.   But who was to save the State,
in whose hands was placed its safety?   In the

hands of those whom nature had endowed with
the requisite strength, the warlike passion. Who
were they? The men! Consequently—women
were less able, less privileged, less worthy than
men. This sort of logic develops very naturally
in practice, even if it is not expressly established,
and the "right of the stronger" is the whole
secret of it.

True enough, women who distinguished themselves by their intellect or virtue were highly
respected among the Athenians, and the appreciation of the most excellent of men was assured
them. But the Aspasias were not numerous, even
in Athens, and such exceptions as social life
offered did not mitigate the unfavorable position in which the law and public opinion placed
woman. Already the classification which was
made of them (as partly also of men) can give an
idea of how dependent and devoid of rights they
were. They consisted, as we know, of three classes,
the slaves, the freed women (out of which class
the courtesans generally were recruited), and the
free born Athenian ladies. It is self-evident that
the first two classes occupied a subordinate position also with regard to the last class. But with
regard to the men even these free born ladies
were semi-slaves. The laws of Solon furnish the
best estimate of their position. They acknowledge
neither any right nor any inclination on the part
of the woman. Fathers, brothers, and guardians

could promise their daughters, sisters, and wards to whom they pleased. The relatives of rich heiresses had a legal right to ask them in marriage, in order that the riches might remain in the family. If a man died childless, his nearest relatives were entitled to his property. Women, daughters and sisters, who were discovered in a dishonorable act, could be sold as slaves by their fathers and brothers. Irregularities on the part of men were, by the way, not considered as adultery. Solon says: " Take a single legitimate, free born daughter for your wife, in order to beget children." With this he exhausted his whole conception of marriage and conjugal morality. He might have said: " According to our laws and ideas, the begetting of legitimate children is limited to the marriage relation between the man and the free born woman ; aside from this, however, the man can keep as many concubines as he likes. But the woman would have to pay for any outside love affair with her liberty or her life."

It was also customary for a time, among the Athenians, to lend their wives. Thus even Socrates is said to have lent his Xantippe to Alkibiades, for which, indeed, according to the reports that are current about this lady, he may not have had need of great self-denial.

These, with regard to women, truly barbaric Solonic laws originated for the most part in patri-

archal conceptions. According to these, among
other things, marriages were allowed inside the
family, in case they were sanctioned or ordered
by the patriarch ; and the power of the head of the
family was so great that the father could decide
over the life or death of his new-born children, or
could deprive them completely of all family rights.

It is of interest to take note here of the view the
Greek writers held of women and their position,
as well as of marriage. I will, therefore, inter-
pose a few significant passages, not indeed from
the poets, but from political and philosophical
prose writers.

Demosthenes says very briefly and with a true
Solonic spirit: "The married woman is an instrument for the procreation of legitimate children
and the management of the household." The
cynical, statesmanlike disdain to which the greatest orator gives utterance in these words throws a
very clear light on the then existing conceptions
of the rights and dignity of woman. Demosthenes stands on a level with Diogenes, who called
woman a necessary evil.

Thucydides is of the opinion that "those wives
deserve the highest praise of whom neither good
nor bad is spoken outside of the house"—a domestic plant, so to speak, a vegetating stay-at-home,
who will serve her husband as an instrument as
well as possible, but is not to concern herself about
anything else. This sentiment of Thucydides has

often since been echoed, and those who did so have entirely overlooked that they repeated in one word a stupidity and a barbarity.

Xenophon thinks rather humanely of women, but still they appear to him as beings whom men, out of regard or pity, must take into their care. He thus expressed his opinion of their inferiority in his " Symposium ": " Zeus has left the women whom he had loved behind him in the class of the mortals, but the men to whom he was devoted he exalted among the gods." Perhaps this proof admits of a refutation by the gallantry that it was no longer necessary to promote lovable women among the gods.

Aristoteles has a higher opinion of woman than Xenophon. He says among other things : " The ruling intelligence is to be attributed to man as the leader. All the other virtues are common to both sexes. Woman is subordinate to man, but still free, and the right to give good counsel (!) cannot be denied her. She furnishes the material which man utilizes."

" Woman is not at all to be regarded as a means for the furtherance of man's selfish ends."

" Husband and wife ought to work together for their support. They go hand in hand, they both accumulate property, their union rests on common benefits and pleasures."

Aristoteles demands that the husband should stake his possessions and his life in the defence of his wife, and should stand by her faithfully and firmly unto death. With regard to chastity he imposes the same obligation on the husband as on the wife.

Most of all, Plato occupied himself with woman. He brings forth much that is contradictory and extravagant. The most important of that which comes under consideration here is condensed in the following, which occasionally gives evidence of so coarse a conception of the sexual relations that it is hard to understand how the poetical Plato could have come by it.

According to him, man and woman share alike in the highest principle, reason, but the powers and capacities under the control of reason are physically as well as psychically weaker in woman, and she is therefore less able to approach perfection, which is the result of the harmony of all forces. (The logic of this proof can perhaps be made plain by the following example. The hawk and the dove are both equally intelligent, but the beak and the claws of the dove are much weaker than those of the hawk. It follows that the dove is less perfect as a dove than the hawk is as a hawk.) It is clear that Plato does not apply the human or feminine standard to the qualities of woman, but the masculine, a senseless presumption which even to-day inspires the judgment of most men. Plato's point of view is shown even still more plainly in the fancy (in the " Phædrus ") that men who have led a dissolute life are changed into women after death—a poor compliment to the sex of whom Goethe says : " The eternal womanly draws us on."

In the " Republic," moreover, Plato says : " Women are physically somewhat weaker than men, but they are otherwise equally adapted to all occupations. In order that they may become able to use all their faculties they must receive the same education as boys, join in the common exercises, not modestly cover up their bodies, etc., etc. I demand the same end and aim for women as for men." (It remains only for Plato to declare it to be the end and aim of woman to become a man. Perhaps it is he who has brought about the mistaken view that it is the purpose of the emancipation of woman to deny femininity and to imitate men.) For the rest, women must be entirely common property, no woman can belong to a single individual. (Thus women are the absolute property of the men.) Moreover, no son is allowed to know a particular father. All must dine together publicly and live together. The State—and that is the *non plus ultra* of brutality—officially brings about the pairing of such persons as it deems the most fit for the procreation of children. When generation has taken place they separate again (a regular institution of stirpiculture). The children are reared by the State without being known by their mothers, so that these sometimes

nurse their own, sometimes the children of others
in the common nursery. In the " Republic " of
Plato there is no private property and no private
interest. He is the grandsire of the communists.
In another place he advocates different principles.

The above extracts show that even the most
excellent writers of the most humane people of
history have not attained to an entirely worthy
conception, to an entirely free view, and to complete justice with regard to the nature and position of woman. Even Aristotle, who, among all,
has laid down the most worthy principles, reaches,
as it were, only a constitutional point of view,
from which he concedes to woman an " advisory "
counsel to governing man and a share in the
" property," without even thinking of such a thing
as an independent right for her. She is considered everywhere only as the property or appendage of man, nowhere as a sovereign being. They
all judge woman only from the standpoint of
men, statesmen, Greeks, not as human beings.
But woman is the genuine representative of the
purely human which must not be modified by
State relations and nationalities.

When Greek liberty had vanished, the regard
for women and the taste for "adoring" them increased. But this adoration was false, and a
product of degenerate conditions. Men had no
longer their former importance, consequently
women came to be more equal to them; men

were now no longer occupied as much with the State, consequently they could devote themselves more to women ; men were now deprived of their public calling, consequently they looked for compensation in the domestic world. Thus also as playthings of the courts and favorites of despots, women are offered rich opportunities in monarchies to achieve a false importance through intrigues and in the relation of mistresses. Upon them falls the favor of the despot, and from them glory and favors radiate downwards. Thus the exaltation of women naturally has for its opposite pole the humiliation of men, and these, in such humiliation, as naturally transform their former contempt of women into that extravagant love-cult and senseless gallantry which spread from Alexandria over the Grecian world.

From the Greeks we proceed to the Romans. These treated women in a truly Spartan manner, only with a more glaring stamp of severity and brutality, in accordance with their severe character. In the most flourishing time of the Roman republic woman was little more than the slave of man.* She was completely his property ; he ac-

---

* It was indeed customary at times that the bride had to say upon entering the house of her husband : *ubi tu es cajus, ego caja sum* (that is, Where you are master I am mistress); but this custom seems to have had merely the force of a gallantry. Its very existence, that is, the necessity for it, seems to indicate a presumption of the very opposite of that which these words would lead us to believe.

quired her through actual purchase or prescription. Whatever she had or earned belonged to him. He could sit in family court over her, and even punish her with death.

Cato, the elder, expresses his respect for the fair sex in these words: "If every head of a family would strive to keep his wife in thorough subjection according to the example of his ancestors, we should have less trouble publicly with the entire sex."

Among the Romans the adulteress could be killed on the spot by her husband; on the part of the man adultery was no crime. Later, however, this was changed. Under Augustus the adultery of the man was punished, as well as that of the woman. It suited the empire in a certain sense to take the side of woman. It may also have been expected that severity toward the degenerate men might prove a means of checking the impending immorality.

Upon the era of the republic followed the era of the emperors and of immorality, perhaps the greatest that ever existed. Men now sought compensation for their lost liberties and for their interrupted political life in all manner of debaucheries, in which the emperors took the lead from sheer *ennui*. For debaucheries, however, women are necessary, and what is necessary is tolerated. The importance to which women attain in eras of immorality can be as little satisfaction to them as that which they are accustomed to have as play-things of the courts. In the age of the Roman emperors, when men were enervated, the importance of woman naturally had to rise. A number of excellent ladies played important rôles at courts and ruled the nations through debauched despots. But this contained no indemnification for the disability of the sex, and that once there has been a Julie, a Messalina, an Agrippina, a Poppæa, a Faustina, etc., can accrue as little to the satisfaction of the feminine sex as the fact that later times have produced a Catherine, a Pompadour, a DuBarry, a Lola, etc.

The reaction against the extravagancies of immorality and sensual debauchery under the Roman emperors was caused by Christianity, by the religion of the man who was not begotten by any man, was born of a virgin, and is said never to have associated with any woman. A religion which referred mankind from the living world to the dead hereafter, which destroyed the value of earthly things, *i.e.*, of reality, and caused humanity to abandon itself to spiritualistic phantasies and reveries, had to put spirituality in place of sensuality, asceticism in place of voluptuousness, and unnatural restraint in place of dissoluteness. Opposing one extreme to another, Christiantity would make nonsense into sense, and a virtue of the violation of nature. If the Romans were immoral through intemperance, the Christians were immoral through abstinence. As regards women in particular, the era of hypocrisy, of the suppression and false conception of their nature, was already announced in the story of the woman who bore a son without the intervention of a man, and in which the functions of the male sex are transferred to doves and ghosts. Christianity, which the priests have made into a paragon of abnormity and hypocrisy, is a real war-sermon against the recognition of the feminine sex, for that which makes woman truly woman Christianity regards for the most part with disgust. Even though Christ pardoned adulteresses and Magdalens, the story of his origin, his abstinence morality, his promises of heaven, and the consequences of Mosaic barbarism which permeate Christianity (it is disgusting to treat these things at large *), have prepared a lot for woman which can only be traced to a suppression of nature, want of sense, and barbarity.

These monstrous teachings, which in the first place caused men to shun woman, logically led to her persecution and maltreatment during the rise of barbarism in the Middle Ages. In the Council of Macon (in the sixth century) a long dispute

---

* Whoever reads the Old Testament as a believing Christian, and notes how woman was created from the rib of man, will easily learn to look upon her not only as the supplement, but also as the property, of man. What man would not consider himself as having a claim upon the product of his rib?

took place (in spite of Adam's rib) whether wom-
en were human beings.   This may give an idea of
the then prevailing Christian view and humane
feeling.   Although the humanity of women was
thus called into doubt, it came gradually to be
recognized in secret with so much zeal, that in
spite of Christianity, the immorality of the tenth
and eleventh centuries reached a degree far ex-
ceeding that of the Roman emperors, perhaps for
the very reason that it was characterized alike by
the most disgusting hypocrisy and the most pious
vulgarity.   However eagerly they were sought
for, women were, in Christian delicacy and appre-
hension, invested with something unclean and un-
holy ; the unfortunate ones were even deprived the
pleasure of touching the altar-cloth, and it was
imposed upon them as a duty to wear gloves at
communion.   Because they could not dispense
with them, they avenged themselves for the sake
of Christianity by degrading them.   Husbands
were permitted by law to beat their wives and
even to inflict wounds on them, provided they did
not disable or maim them thereby.   The father
could chastise his daughter even after her marriage.   In the city of Bourbon a husband could
with impunity kill his wife if he only swore that
he was heartily sorry for it—all this in consequence
of the humane ideas which the unnatural doctrine
had caused that preached an unnatural universal
love of mankind, while it made a crime of the

natural love of the sexes.   The horrors to which
women were subjected in monasteries, priests'
brothels, and courts of inquisition we will entirely
omit.*   On the other hand, we shall attach no importance to the fact that at certain periods of the
Middle Ages single women acquired distinction
as artists, authors, etc.   They acquired it, so to
speak, merely as a reflex of monastic life.   They
were regarded as *nuns,* not as *women.*

After Christian contempt and abuse of women
had reached the extreme, it began in the twelfth
and thirteenth centuries to retrace its steps to the
other extreme, to glorify them and make them
objects of idolatry.   That brings us to the time
of those noble knights who as highway robbers
at one moment slew their fellow-men, and the
next moment, as sighing paladins, lay on their
knees before their lady-love.   That these moon-
calves even at a later time could be regarded as

* Marriage was only a necessary evil to Christian priests, and
open intercourse of the sexes a horror; thus arose celibacy,
the mode of life of monks, etc.   Some sought to attain to the
loftiest height of the Christian spirit by actually unmanning
themselves ; other priests, on the other hand, indulged their
passions to such an extent that they openly claimed the *jus
primæ noctis,* and enforced it with truly Christian zeal.   Marriages which were consecrated in this manner were thought to
be especially blessed and continually hovered about by the
holy ghost.   After some reflection this seems obvious, and it
would be indeed astonishing if the holy ghost had only once
experienced an inclination to descend to a people who honored
him so gratefully,

models of noble manhood by the ladies, is due to those senseless romanticists who have sought for the spirit of poesy in opposition to reason. Otherwise it would have been obvious to every child that a man made up of vulgarity from top to toe, whose only study consisted in riding and killing, was not capable of any truly noble attachment to woman, even if, through the fashionable exaggeration of a coxcombical gallantry, he should have reached such a stage of eccentricity as to allow himself to be despatched out of the world for the sake of his lady-love. How delicate the sentiments of these heroes were in practice is shown by the fact that when they had to absent themselves from home for the purpose of slaying, they would place a solidly wrought lock on the adored body of their " noble lady " in order to facilitate her leading a chaste life.

What the knights were as lovers, the minstrels in many respects were as poets of love. The object in view rarely was to give poetic expression of real sentiments which could bear the test of reason, but as a rule only the versified exaggeration of an artificial emotion, in order to satisfy the prevailing fashion. Thus as gallantry and killing were the stereotyped modes of amusement, so the poetical praise of these arts was also treated as an entertaining handicraft. Women could not find a true recognition and appreciation in an age when men sought their highest honor in throwing each other from the horse, or in other ways breaking each other's necks.

At a later period the position of woman in France especially claims our attention. There, according to the national character, chivalry took on a more spiritual expression and a more graceful form, and from the chivalrous gallantry which inspired the Duke de la Rochefoucault with the verses (on Madame de Longueville):

> Pour mériter son cœur,
> Pour plaire à ses beaux yeux
> J'ai fait la guerre aux rois,
> Je l'aurais faite aux dieux—

love for women passed through various phases of fastidiousness and frivolity till it reached that bright relationship in which the "beautiful" and "strong" minds of the Ninons and their lovers at the time found their greatest happiness. But also this relationship, upon which the reflection of court-life so often cast its splendor, and which can furnish no standard for the average position of women, rarely was an entirely true and satisfactory one, and was moreover confined only to certain circles. Through it a sphere was opened only for social life in which women had to seek compensation for the deprivations of political life, while complete political and social liberty must form, as it were, the atmosphere in which the flower of love unfolds itself.

In the French revolution no definite position could be developed for women. They indeed played a great part in it, just as the French nation possesses the most excellent women, but even in France the theoretical and historical preparations, which could become the foundation for a new position of the weaker sex, were wanting ; moreover the revolutionary struggle very soon changed into the history of Napoleonic "heroism" in which the women of course were forced into the background before soldiers and weapons. The soldier has no other position for women than that of whores or daughters of the regiment.

After the Napoleonic period, women as well as men, as we know, spent their days in a condition of vacillation, unconsciousness, prostitution, and philistinism. The position of women can still be designated by three words : they are tolerated, used, and protected so far and so long as men see fit, and must always remain about as far behind them in their demands and their progress as their physical strength remains behind that of the men. Although, after passing through Antiquity and the Middle Ages, time has developed more humane customs and forms, women, in relation to men or in comparison with men, are still without rights in almost every respect ; and in a thousand cases where a man may and can emancipate himself, emancipation for woman remains a crime and an impossibility. The history of women up to this time can therefore in reality only be a history of their disqualification, and it need not astonish us that men have refrained from writing it. The greater need of freedom which women themselves are manifesting indicates a step in progress. In no age have there been so many women who have demanded the emancipation of their sex as in ours, and that is the first requisite to the attainment of emancipation. First of all it is necessary to make women generally conscious of the need of emancipation, and to spread clear views not only in regard to existing injustice, but also in regard to the justice that is to be acquired.

The position of women is to-day, as always, closely connected with the entire network of the political, social, economic, and religious conditions. It is therefore necessary to examine the various aims and conditions of the emancipation of women, which the following treatise proposes to do by means of a brief review of prevailing opinions and circumstances. Above all things the general aim and province of the emancipation with regard to the nature and lot of woman must be considered in a few words.

THE EMANCIPATION OF WOMAN.

THE emancipation of woman has been greatly ridiculed, and partly with good reason. It is generally understood in a way that involves a misconception of woman's lot, a repudiation of the feminine nature, and an ambition to enter the province of the masculine. And this conception (we have found it as early as Plato, as shown in the foregoing chapter) has frequently been provoked or encouraged by women themselves, inasmuch as they sought to manifest their emancipation in the imitation of masculine externalities and in unfeminine display. But the emancipation that is to be considered here has nothing to do with female smokers and with sportswomen, nor with huntresses and amazons, nor with female scholars and bluestockings, nor with female diplomatists and queens. I think it is no offence to women if we consider them as in their proper place only in the manifestations of pure humanity, true culture, and reason. We might otherwise easily come to consider masculine women as the ideal. But there is nothing more repulsive in this world than a masculine woman, even if she should glorify her masculinity with the splendor of a crown. The celebrated Elizabeth of England was

a real monster of a woman, and it is astonishing
that this "virgin" hypocrite found even a single
lover.

In a word, the chief error in the direction of
the emancipation of woman has hitherto consisted in the attempt to educate woman into a
man, and even into a man of the present state of
development, that is, on occasion even into a soldier, instead of vindicating her humanity and her
right to citizenship in accordance with her nature
as against man, and allowing her nature free
scope of development and of activity. Because
hitherto man alone could assert himself, the belief
has arisen that the self-assertion of woman must
begin on masculine domain. But with this sort
of emancipation the feminine sex is benefited
least of all. Let us but imagine the opposite
case, namely, that the oppressed man is to be
emancipated by a feminine education and by being
assigned a feminine sphere of action. Without a
true conception of and strict adherence to the
feminine nature, every attempt at emancipation
must necessarily lead to error and absurdity. We
hear many a woman express the wish that she
were a man. Not one of them would ever strike
upon such unnatural wishes of despair, if she had
the opportunity and liberty of being entirely a
woman.

If the woman oversteps the limits of her nature
and destiny, she does not find an elevated stand-

point in her thought upon which she could place
herself. A man, if he attempts to soar beyond
his sphere, at least finds in his imagination the
aggrandizement and glorification which endow
him with a superhuman character : he is called a
"giant," a "demon," a "god." But the woman,
if she breaks through her circle, does not find a
higher stage than that which the aspiring man
has *left behind*, and she never attains to anything
more than being the imitator of—man. The
man, if he overleaps, loses at most his name, the
woman also her sex. The woman can become a
"god" or "goddess" only when she aspires to be
only a woman. Growth by means of masculine
qualities makes a monster of woman. We men
have nothing to surrender to you women by
which you could improve, beautify, and ennoble
yourselves; everything good, beautiful, and noble
you possess in your truly humane hearts, your
fine feeling, and your susceptible minds. *Inter*-
change our qualities we can and must, *ex*change
them, never !

When we speak of the emancipation of woman,
the point cannot therefore be to obscure the sexual limits. These limits should and must, rather,
be strictly retained, but defined in such a manner
that the man cannot infringe on the domain of
woman arbitrarily. The woman is not to be his
prisoner, his slave, and his tool, and he not her
guardian, her master, and her exploiter.

Hitherto woman has only been looked upon as a supplement and appendage to man. *The human being* per se, *the independent personality, the soverreign individual has never been recognized in woman.* It seems that the Bushmen on the Cape of Good Hope are the only ones who have considered woman equal to man, for they have only one expression for both. The woman is to belong to the man; the question, why is not the man likewise to belong to the woman, occurs to no one. She is brought up for the man, and must live for the man; she receives her name from the man; she is "taken" by the man, supported by the man, put under obligation to the man, made the ward of the man, punished by the man, used by the man, and forsaken by the man.

The man is considered as a human being, the woman as only the appendix to this human being; but the woman is more a human being than the present man, and human rights know no sex. As a certain French orator said that law is an atheist, it can be said of right that it is a neuter. But hitherto right has always been of the male sex. Men have made the rights, men have made the morals, men have made the duties, men have made the laws, and they have taken good care that woman should be excluded as much as possible from everything.

But, it will be said, you have declared that the limits of womanhood must be adhered to, and yet

you wish from the start to introduce woman into
the sphere of men ?   This is only apparently done.
Woman is to participate in public and political
life only as far as is consistent with her nature ;
but if *public and political life, has hitherto been so
coarse and violent that only masculine nature and
strength could perform the chief work in it*, it
neither follows for the past that the smaller part
the more delicate nature of woman could necessarily have played in public life *ought to have furnished a standard for her human rights*, nor does
it follow for the future that the work of public
and political life will always *remain so coarse and
violent as it has been until now*, and that therefore
the participation of woman in the same *must always meet with the same difficulties.*

The chief work of history, that coarse prelim-
inary work which has so far called for the greatest strength, and the purely male qualities, but
which at the same time, to the disgrace of reason
be it said, gave these qualities their most glorious
significance, has hitherto beeñ *wholesale murder*,
war.   This work could of course not be performed
by the women ; but neither could the successes,
the fame, and the merit of it fall to their lot.
The men carried on this murderous profession
alone, had to carry it on alone according to their
nature, and whatever the women did in the mean-
time, according to *their* nature, was not credited
to them as worthy of the same distinction as mur-

der was to the men. The women were therefore
neglected and disqualified because they did not—
murder. Let us imagine history without war, or
the weaker sex capable of engaging in war, and
*the entire position of woman is changed in an in-
stant.* Among warlike nations the woman was
least valued, and the abolition of war is the liberation of woman.

At bottom it is therefore chiefly the preponderance of physical strength and of the warlike passion which gives man the right to lay exclusive
claim to public and political life. Not alone in war,
but also in other branches of public and political
work these same qualities are more or less required,
so that whithersoever we look, physical strength
and the warlike passion, which is wanting in
woman, play an important part. But is there
here any equitable warrant for considering women
less qualified as human beings and as citizens?
Does right depend on the size of the gall-blad-
der, on the strength of the limbs, on the thickness
of the bones, on the hardness of the muscles, or
the coarseness of the fists? And could not the
woman be granted the right to "counsel" even
where she was incapable of "acting"? Was it therefore necessary to deprive her of all rights where
she was immediately concerned and entirely com-
petent? Because the woman cannot lead an
army in the field, may she therefore not have any
voice in her own affairs? Because a woman can-

not be a policeman, shall therefore a husband be
allowed to have her brought back into his house
by policemen when she has escaped from him, he
having become unbearable? Because a woman
cannot become a sheriff, may a sheriff therefore
tear away from her the children whom she has
borne, and return them to the hated father who
will maltreat them? Because a woman perhaps
cannot be a minister of finance, must the man
therefore be her financial guardian? Because a
woman is less fitted for a scholar and philosopher,
shall education therefore be forbidden ground to
her? Because a woman, in a word, *cannot be a
man*, must she therefore be less a human being
and a citizen than man? I admit that besides
the physical strength and the warlike passion there
are still other qualities of mind and character
which in a hundred situations capacitate the man
for the work of history where the woman is un-
able to act. But this can affect the *rights* of
woman all the less since her sphere, in a purely
human respect, is infinitely richer in service to
society than that of the men. At all events, they
must have the same right to develop and to exercise their faculties in every direction, according to
their own desires.

Democrats maintain that the dignity and the
right of man consist in his self-determination,
and that he is to obey only those laws in the
making of which he himself has participated. But

do the laws of the State only concern men ? Why should the women obey laws which were made without their aid ? Are there " human dignity" and " self-determination " for men and not for women ? Millions of women suffer under the oppression of shameful marriage laws, and women are to be excluded from the deliberation of such laws? Is a law which men dictate to women less an act of violence than the law a despot dictates to men? Whether the men deprive the woman of her rights in a democratic assembly, or whether a despot does the same to the man in his cabinet, amounts to one and the same thing from the standpoint of right ; and when a so-called government, having, through all possible means, kept the people in a state of ignorance, declares them to be not ripe for liberty, this declaration is just as justifiable as when the men keep the women in a state of helplessness and on that account judge them incapable of participation in political life. So long, therefore, as the women have not equal political and civil rights with the men, in order to assert themselves so far as their ability and their interest prompt them, there is still a great deal wanting in the logic of democrats. The opinions of a man about women can quite properly be considered as the measure of his qualification for liberty and humanity. Whoever is 'not just towards women preaches vulgarity and adopts despotism. Daily experience also teaches that those most distinguish themselves by intellectual and moral vulgarity who treat the emancipation of women with scorn or condemnation.

First, therefore, comes the political emancipation of woman, *i.e.*, her installation into her political rights, so that she may have the liberty and the opportunity to guard her own interests in the State without the tutelage of the men.

Besides this emancipation, however, there is still the conventional, the moral, the economic, the religious, etc., to be aspired to, the object of which must always be only to establish the liberty and the right of women within the limits prescribed by the feminine nature, and to protect them against the invasions and the commands of men, or to abolish woman's dependence on the will of the men, and finally also to place woman in a position to freely act out her true nature by means of every aid.

These different points will be discussed in detail in the following pages. It is to be observed that political emancipation is the chief point at issue as against men, even in the freest, while, for instance, religious emancipation, economic emancipation, are questions which remain to be solved even for the majority of the male sex, almost everywhere, and are therefore more of a common concern. In respect to women, however, every single question takes on a special shape, wherefore it may be worth while to consider each one singly.

It has been intimated before that the liberty and influence of women must grow in the same degree in which the brutal strength of men declines in value. The nearer, therefore, the time approaches when decisions through force are replaced by decisions based on right, when wars are abolished as barbarities, when the strength of the hands is directed only against nature, and even in that struggle has in a great measure become superfluous through the skill of machinery, etc., the more will the man approach the humane plane upon which the woman, so to speak, stands waiting until the savage has become appeased, and has developed the capacity of acknowledging a being as free and endowed with rights, who is wanting the strength to enforce its liberty and its rights. Woman represents, as it were, from the start the humane principle, and man in a certain sense becomes a human being only in so far as he approaches woman. A great part of that which hitherto has passed as "manly" is nothing more than barbarity. Brutal strength, which has been a mere means in the pioneer work of history, has come to be considered as a principle and as a permanent object. Thus what has been looked upon as the highest will hereafter be declared to be the lowest, and women will have to learn that many a "hero" whom they have adored as the ideal of manliness, at a later time will appear as a murderer or a rowdy.

From these suggestions, concerning the natural way in which even history in part leads woman on towards emancipation, it does, however, by no means follow that woman is to look towards the future in a mere attitude of expectancy. It is, on the contrary, necessary to strive in all directions that women, through participation in the struggles of the times, should come to the aid of emancipating history, and it is moreover essential to stir up their sense of justice and their moral sense by contact with even the most disgusting phases of life. They will thus acquire a complete survey of their position and their claims. From this point of view the following chapters are especially to be judged.

THE PASSIVE PROSTITUTION OF WOMEN.

WOMAN has, in advance of man, the bitter satisfaction that there is a far greater chasm between
the different positions which she occupies in poetry and in life than between all the positions which
can be imagined for a male being. Worshipped
as an ideal in poetry, degraded below the animal
in life, woman may contemplate how much resti-
tution must be made to her in order to fill out the
chasm between her degradation and her apotheosis.
Indeed, between the most exalted man of history or
the drama, and the lowest slave of the bagnio or the
plantation, there is not so great a contrast by far
as between a Laura or Heloïse and a prostitute of
the street or the brothel.

Woman has a double task of liberation. First
she bears with man the common yoke of the prevailing oppression ; but if this yoke is cast off,
there still remains for her the special yoke which
the male sex has placed on her neck. In the man
the *human being* alone can be oppressed or liber-
ated, in the woman the sex as well.

The despot makes a slave of the man by oppression, but even this slave makes a sub-slave of
the woman by purchase. Even for the slave the

possibility of saving the better self is still conceivable.   But a woman in a state of prostitution
is both a slave and a human monstrosity at the
same time.   The woman is born for love, and
drowns her heart in a bog of vice; the woman is
born for motherhood, and to be a mother becomes
a horror to her; the woman is born to be a wife,
and of the happiness of a wife she has never any
conception.   Thus is the woman in a state of
prostitution.   Surely, to sell one's "love" without
choice and without love is the lowest stage of
human abjectness.   If all women could feel the
degradation which is the lot of millions of their
sex in the state of prostitution, the whole sex
would rise in rebellion and begin a sex war, as
there have hitherto been national and religious
wars.

The way in which woman has reached this
degradation also indicates the way to free herself
from it.   First came force, which compelled the
woman to give herself even to the man she most
despised.   As a slave, and as an ornament to the
harem, she was in the beginning mere booty.
The preponderance of physical strength, force,
was the immediate cause that made woman a
tool, a thing without rights.   This force was con-
verted, also with respect to the men, into political
power, the power of princes, and as such became
at the same time an object of veneration.   The
men honored it as subjects, the women as tools of

lust.   The honor which a woman supposes to be done her when a despot chooses her for his mistress is nothing more than a continuation of the subserviency with which formerly the slave would surrender herself to the murderer.

First made dependent on man through force, the woman fell into twofold dependence as growing civilization made the maintenance of existence more difficult.   Woman existed not only *for* the man, but also *through* man, who by virtue of his physical strength and his energetic mind found the way to procure the means of existence and of luxury.   And when civilization reached a height where the inequality in the economic conditions was so far developed that even a great part of the men could procure none or insufficient means of existence and of luxury, that part of the feminine sex which was dependent on them became completely helpless, completely dependent.   The helpless woman, thrown upon herself by the helpless man, but through education and circumstances alike incapacitated to help herself, gave up the only thing she possessed : she sold her body.   She sold it first from hunger, then to get means for luxury and amusement.   And this lot, originally prepared by force and then decided upon by necessity, has now become an actual profession for millions.   Prostitution has become a true branch of industry, which has its employers and contractors, as well as its science and its articles

of trade. It is at the same time a hereditary corruption which is transmitted from the mother to
the children, and pursues entire classes from one
generation to the other, inasmuch as the want of
means for existence goes hand in hand with the
want of means for education.

Out of regard for the weaker nerves of women
(since women have weaker nerves than men), I
shall refrain from picturing in detail the fate to
which so many thousands, especially in great
cities, among them a great part in the most tender
age of virginity, are consigned. Whatever the
imagination can conceive as low and disgusting,
that is suffered, is cultivated by a great part of
the feminine sex from necessity, and for money.
Every hesitation which the feelings or the sensual
impressions might oppose in a single case is
overcome by necessity and by money ; and we may
not be far from the truth in imagining the most
beautiful and lovable girl in the world transferred
to the chambers of a brothel, where she trem-
blingly begins the practice of her profession in the
arms of a decrepit old man, whose aspect causes
all the five senses at once to revolt, but whom
money enables to stimulate his deadened vitality
by means of a youthful beauty for—a double
premium.

But now, you women who shudder at the reading of such things, do you believe that prostitution is to be found only in those haunts where a

tax is levied on every act of lust? Look about you in your social ranks and you will find that the circle of prostitution encloses thousands of families who make the sign of the cross at the mention of the word brothel. When a girl marries from necessity, or is made to marry from speculation, is not that as much prostitution as when she sells herself from necessity or is sold from speculation? To be sure, by marriage she sells herself only to a single person, but that does not change the immorality of her relationship. Those women who can still say a year after their marriage that their husbands are really the men of their hearts are indeed rare, at least among certain classes; and this confession is nothing more than a confession of prostitution. Most marriages are the product of money or class considerations, or exigencies to avoid in the eleventh hour the entire failure of the sexual design. But where marriage as a rule is a mere charitable institution, it at once becomes by law also an institution of compulsion, which perpetuates prostitution and makes regret useless.

No further exposition is necessary to show that the sources of prostitution, into which the greater part of the feminine sex has fallen, are political disqualification and economic dependence, *i.e.*, the twin tyranny which throws the greatest part of humanity under the feet of the ruling, revelling minority. The abolition of prostitution is possible, therefore, only after the attainment of complete liberty and after the just regulation of the social conditions, of which we shall speak farther on. But pious vulgarity and the moral police are of a different opinion. They think that they stifle prostitution at its source if they drive the unhappy inmates of houses of ill-fame out of town with police force or throw them into prison. It is dreadful that history necessitates more victims of ignorance than enlightenment, when at last attained, is able to make happy beings. How many millions will have perished in misery and degradation before the knowledge has at last been reached that neither the police nor church discipline are able to banish an evil which is the necessary result of legal and economic conditions! And what is easier than this knowledge if we are willing to abandon the obstinacy of our egotism with the slothfulness of our thinking?

THE ACTIVE PROSTITUTION OF MEN.

LET us begin with the education of men. By education I do not here mean mere domestic and school education, but also the sum of all other influences of life which determine the intellectual and moral development of man to the time of complete independence.

Generally even in the beginning of the period when sexual uneasiness begins to show itself in the boy, he is exposed in schools, institutes, and elsewhere to the temptations of secret vice, which is transmitted from youth to youth like a contagious corruption, and which in thousands destroys the first germs of virility. A countless number of boys is addicted to these vices for years. That they do not in the beginning of nascent puberty proceed to sexual intercourse with women, which would, by the way, be in every respect less injurious, is generally due to youthful timidity, which dares not reveal its desire, or from want of experience for finding opportunities. Only too often this timidity and this want are overcome by chance or by seduction, which is rarely lacking in great cities where prostitution is flourishing, and thus numbers of boys immediately after the transition period of youth, in accordance with the previous secret practice, accustom themselves to the association with prostitute women. At the age when European youths are put into the soldier's uniform or are wont to enter the university, this association frequently becomes an object of boasting, and to calm the sexual desires in a pool of filth and, in connection with it, to undermine health by intemperance or disgusting diseases, is generally developed into a fine art in soldier and student life.

Thus prepared, the young man approaches the time when he can seriously think of making the acquaintance of a girl who as his wife is to satisfy his heart and his sexual needs. Most men of the educated classes enter the marriage-bed with the consciousness of leaving behind them a whole army of prostitutes or seduced women in whose arms they cooled their passions and spent the vigor of their youth. But with this past the married man does not at the same time leave behind him its influence on his inclinations. The habit of having a feminine being at his disposal for every rising appetite, and the desire for change inordinately indulged for years, generally make themselves felt again as soon as the honeymoon is over. The satisfaction which an uncorrupted man could find in the arms of his wife for many years is shortened all the more for the man of the common sort, the more he has learned to look upon woman as a mere instrument for the satisfaction of his changeable sexual appetite. For the simple reason, moreover, that women are to be had for the asking, most men do not know how to appreciate them. Thousands of men have before marriage lost the capacity of entering into a sincere or moral relation, and give their wives nothing but their name.

A new epoch now begins for the married man, the epoch of conjugal deception. What he had formerly done almost publicly he now does secretly, and often at an incredible expense of hypocrisy and cunning. Very few women in the least suspect the dissipations of their husbands, and I know not whether it is for their good that they suspect nothing. In Paris, to be sure, women generally know how they stand with their husbands, and they know also how to provide against being pitied.

If all men were to write Rousseauian Confessions concerning their secret sexual doings, the greater part of the educated women would be driven to despair or turn away from the male sex in disgust. Not a few of those married men who formerly associated with courtesans because they had no wives now address themselves to their wives only when they have no courtesans.

Now, although most men are in a certain sense "not worthy to unloose the latchet of the shoes" of the commonest woman, much less to "unfasten her girdle," yet they make the most extravagant

demands on the feminine sex.   Even the greatest
debauchee, who has spent his vigor in the arms
of a hundred courtesans, will cry out fraud and
treachery if he does not receive his newly married
bride as an untouched virgin.   Even the most
dissolute husband will look on his wife as deserving of death if his daily infidelity is only once
reciprocated.   And while he demands that his
wife should remain faithful because her nature
requires it, he will nevertheless involve himself in
the contradiction of always suspecting this nature
of a tendency to unfaithfulness because he trans-
fers his own experiences and weaknesses to the
woman.   Thus he not only deceives his wife, he
also even punishes her for deceiving her.   But,
himself always jealous without cause, he will be
indignant at the most justifiable jealousy on the
part of his wife.   A husband who is annoyed by
the jealousy of his wife deserves it—and what
husband is not annoyed by it?   No husband can
bring his concessions into any proportion with his
demands, and nowhere does this show itself more
plainly than in jealousy.   While he asks of his
wife to take precautions against even the appearance of misdemeanors of which she has never
thought, he on his part claims freedom from reproach for all offences of the past and the future.

   We are frequently severe towards others only
because we have not yet had an opportunity to
commit their offences.   We are wont to become

all the more magnanimous the more cause we have to depend on the magnanimity of others. Of this truth not an iota is corroborated where the views of men with respect to women are concerned. The greater the injustice a husband does to his wife, the less is he willing to submit to from her; the oftener he becomes unfaithful to her, the stricter he is in demanding faithfulness from her. We see that despotism nowhere denies its own nature: the more a despot deceives and abuses his people, the more submissiveness and faithfulness he demands of them.

Who can be astonished at the many unhappy marriages, if he knows how unworthy most men are of their wives! Their virtues they rarely can appreciate, and their vices they generally call out by their own. Thousands of women suffer from the results of a mode of life of which they, having remained pure in their thought, have no conception whatever; and many an unsuspecting wife nurses her husband with tenderest care in sicknesses which are nothing more than the consequences of his *amours* with other women. And when at last, after long years of delusion and endurance, the scales drop from the eyes of the wife, and revenge or despair drives her into a hostile position towards her lord and master, she is an inhuman criminal, and the hue and cry against the fickleness of women and the falsity of their nature is endless.

On an average, men, married as well as unmarried, are so constituted that they will not easily let slip an opportunity of secretly entering into sexual relations with any woman who can excite their senses. And it generally requires very little to excite their senses. Those that are insatiable are in certain respects as easily to be satisfied as they are insatiable. This sexual inclination of men, be it in consequence of their education or by nature, is so constant and general that most of them view every woman they meet only with the reflection whether she would be likely to enter into relations with them or not. While the sight of a man inspires them with questions after his business, his views, his intellect, etc., that of a woman causes them only, or directly, to speculate on her sexual willingness. There you see a statesman, a clergyman, or an official—all people who in the presence of others distinguish themselves by a serious and severe demeanor which would lead us to suspect almost anything else than an illicit sentiment towards women ; personages who inspire respect, living laws, embodied sermons, walking documents. The serious statesman, or clergyman, or official meets a pretty lady or a pretty servant-girl on a promenade where the eyes of the world or of his acquaintances are not upon him. In passing he will look intently and lustfully into her eyes, and if she only half reciprocates his look, or only answers with a humane smile, an object on the way, or a bird in the trees, or the beauty of the surroundings, in short anything, will suddenly attract his attention and give him in the eyes of a casual passer-by an excuse for looking round after her. And if she looks round also, he will have forgotten his handkerchief or something else which will necessitate his following her in order to convince himself that he may, in a *tête-à-tête,* exchange the serious statesman, clergyman, or official for an unmasked member of the male sex. Every look of a woman, caused perhaps only by curiosity or thoughtlessness or good-nature, exposes her at once with common men to the danger of an appearance of common coquetry, or the suspicion of sensual desire. Every pretty or even agreeable-looking woman who travels alone, or crosses the street alone in the evening, will find occasion to ward off importunities. The reputation of many a woman is endangered merely by the fact that she does not regulate her behavior in accordance with an entirely low conception of men, that she does not think she is throwing herself away by being natural, that she has not accustomed herself to see a crime in candor. Thus are most men restlessly pursued by the instinct and fancies of sensuality! Any man will, under safe conditions, put himself at the disposal of any pretty woman, if she desires nothing more than sensual pleasure. There are be few physically healthy men who can give the lie to this sentence.

The habit of regarding the end and aim of woman only from the most vulgar side—not to respect in her the noble human being, but to see in her only the instrument of sensual desire—is carried so far among men that they will allow it to force into the background considerations among themselves which they otherwise pretend to rank very high ; for instance the considerations of friendship.   There are few men who are so faithful in their friendship that they would scruple to put the fidelity of the pretty wife of their friend to the test.   Adultery through so-called friends of the family is the most common of all.   Love and horse-trading are two articles in which, among a great many men, deceit appears to be legitimate and seems to be taken into the bargain in " friendship."

From all these hidden parts of our social relations the paint must be washed off.   Women must become indignant ; and if I had not sufficient confidence in them to think the above will suffice, I could sketch a far more glaring picture, without laying myself open to the charge of exaggeration.

But when the feeling of women has once been driven to indignation with respect to the position which they occupy, it is to be hoped that they will only the more urgently look for a way to attain a worthier position, and to follow that way, when it is found, with persistence.

THE EXCUSES OF MEN.

IN the previous chapter I have dwelt on the sins against women which our sex commits through prostitution. In order to be just towards both sides I shall also point out the circumstances which for the present may still serve to excuse men, although not to justify them.

The sexual instinct is as natural and as legitimate as the instinct for eating and drinking. Whatever nature demands cannot and should not be denied her ; it is only necessary to find the ethical rules which will secure the satisfaction of the natural needs without involving degeneration.

Whatever is unnatural is also immoral. But it is unnatural, consequently immoral, that circumstances will not allow a man after having reached puberty to follow his natural instincts and to associate himself with a woman. If it were possible to the youth to marry young, he would, at the hand of his beloved, pass by all the moral cesspools through which the unmarried are driven by the passion of their sexual instinct. He would not have to go through those schools of corruption in which he learns to fit himself for everything which later makes him unfit for any true conjugal relation. In the arms of his beloved he would preserve the health which he poisons in the arms of the harlot. He would respect women, because he would not have had the opportunity of making their acquaintance in the most contemptible of all states, and his untainted mind would not change into that unscrupulousness which, as Jean Paul says, does not hesitate to pluck to pieces the noblest woman like a bee, only for the sake of getting hold of the honey-sack.

With all our civilization we are put to shame even by the savages. The savages know of no fastidiousness of the sexual instinct and of no brothels, because their nature need do no violence to itself and can satisfy its needs in a natural manner. They show us at the same time that health, as well as morals, is less endangered when nature is allowed free play than when it is driven into by-ways through obstacles.

We are, indeed, likewise savages, but in quite a different sense. Proof of this is especially furnished by our youth. But that our students, and young men in general, usually pass through the school of corruption and drag the filth of the road which they have traversed before marriage along with them throughout life, is not their fault so much as the fault of prejudices and of our political and social conditions. Nature demands, as has been said, the satisfaction of the sexual instinct when the age of puberty has been reached.

Our priests, moral teachers, and schoolmasters, great and small, maintain, however, that nature is a vicious, disqualified person whose demands must be rejected until they, the priests, etc., shall grant her a hearing, and mark her with the stamp of official approbation. That through this rejection ten times the evil is brought about which these wise gentlemen pretend to avoid, they themselves know very well; but if there is no more censorship the censors will lose their bread and butter.

Our political and social conditions conform to the prejudices sustained by our religious and moral falsifiers. Partly through police limitations, partly through the degeneration of our economic conditions, most men are prevented from marrying until the uneasiest period of their sexual life is passed. Yes, thousands, especially among our idling military, are not able to support a wife until they are almost old men, and after they have for half a lifetime been masters in the school of debauchery and seduction; and as concerns the thousands of priests whom celibacy compels to revenge oppressed nature with hypocrisy and all manner of secret means, I do not know whether the disgust at their loathsome lives or pity for their inhuman lot should furnish the standard by which we should judge them.

Attention must be repeatedly called to the fact that, besides celibacy, student and military life in Europe are the high-schools of prostitution. After the young man for ten years has stood under the lash of pedantic and servile school-masters, he feels himself free for the first time at the university. But it is not the freedom which permits him to develop his mental powers in all directions and to accustom himself to participate in public life; no, he has only the freedom to spend the money of his parents without being watched, and to find in inns and brothels an out-let for his longing to exercise his rising powers. The systematic favoring of these doings seems even to be a part of the plan of the governmental system of instruction, and the wish of high states-manship is fulfilled if the young man leaves the university enervated and dulled; he requires nothing more than ability to pass his exami-nations and to execute the commands of the powers that be. That the powers that be do not consider whether the youth who is used to de-bauchery is still capable of making a wife happy need not astonish the female sex as long as they cannot comprehend the connection between their interests and political development.

The women moreover will admit that the stand-ing armies will not be abolished out of gallantry. For do not the standing armies furnish the chief representatives of gallantry? The powers that be are liberal enough to allow the maltreated soldier and the bored officer to seek compensation for the hardships of their profession among the degraded feminine sex, and the degraded feminine sex is sufficiently grateful to recognize the blessing of having fops instead of men, dancing partners instead of friends, whore-hunters instead of husbands, educated for them by raving about the resplendent soldiery. In Switzerland and North America women must be very unhappy, because men must dispense with the chief school of training for married life, namely, the standing armies! But they are compensated here by the moneyed men, who can buy everything, and by the friends of the slave-holders, who see to it that the doctrine of the despoliation of the weak does not suffer.

But marriage also, as it now exists, is a school for the dissemination of conjugal infelicity for men no less than for women. More of this later. It appears on all sides that most men also are the victims of existing conditions, that is, of the present want of freedom and of economic injustice, whereupon the women become the victims of the victims.

A special point which comparatively admits of an excuse for men in the discussion of sexual rights and duties is, finally, "adultery." The condition for equal claims is equal needs. Now if it can be shown that the woman has the same sexual needs as the man, then adultery on her part is of no greater significance than on the part of man. But whether we find the reason for it in

the difference of education or in the difference of
nature, it can be considered an established fact
that the man is much more liable to sexual temptations than the woman ; or that the mere sensual
need is much less in woman than in the man.   A
further difference follows from the present conjugal conditions.   The man must as a rule take upon
himself the care of the family, and the members
of the family, the children, depend on the head of
the family for the means of existence.   By " adultery," therefore, the wife runs the risk not only of
unjustly increasing the cares of her husband, but
also of lessening the rights of his children,—considerations which the man generally need not overcome in " adultery."   Moreover, an extraordinary
digression on the part of the man, according to
the prevailing and in part justifiable opinions,
does not, when it becomes publicly known, reflect
any disgrace upon the wife—she is rather sympa-
thized with as the suffering, the injured party ;
but a digressing wife exposes her husband to
scorn and contempt.

All these differences and excuses, however, according to which the husband sins less and the
wife more by " adultery," are to be considered as
admissible only from the standpoint of our present conditions.   It will later appear that from a
correct point of view both sexes must be measured by the same standard of right.   Least of
all do I by excusing men intend to accuse women.

I recognize as much the blamelessness of most women who take a false step as the hypocrisy of most men who try to enlarge upon the misdemeanors of women. I even ask the men who would secure the inviolability of female fidelity by referring their wives to the consequences for the family, whether they would grant them the same liberty which they claim for themselves if they knew them to be sterile? The negative answer must here again disclose that Jesuitical egotism which, by using "the right of the stronger," tries to fetter the weaker with forced considerations, in order to secure greater scope for itself, and which tries to magnify the faults of others in order to lessen its own. Should it nevertheless appear desirous to punish the infidelity of women, I would propose capital punishment on condition that the infidelity of the men be punished by Abélardization.

LOVE AND JEALOUSY.

A LADY-FRIEND has requested of me an answer to the following questions:

1. " Is jealousy an inborn or an inbred passion ?"

2. "Can a human being love several persons at once, and if he believes himself able to do this, can this capacity be called love?"

Logic demands that I answer the second question first, for jealousy must be looked at as a concomitant of love, not love as a concomitant of jealousy.

What is love? In simple words : a passionate attachment to a person of the other sex, in whom a man (or woman) delights in the highest degree, and for whom he feels the highest degree of appreciation, confidence, and good-will. Through the highest degree of appreciation, etc., we place the person on an ideal standpoint. The conception of the ideal, however, excludes every second ideal. By the side of an ideal we can as little have another ideal of the same kind as the believer can have another God besides the well-known Universal One.

If we conceive of love as a passionate enthusiasm and devotion to a thereby idealized person, it is self-evident that its object can never be more than one single individual at the same time. "Thou entirely fillest my soul,"* sings the poet, and a full soul has as little room for other contents as a full bottle of champagne.

But now it happens very frequently in this queer world which denies to most people the opportunity of entering into suitable relations, or the liberty of dissolving unsuitable connections, that an object of love which "fills the soul entirely" cannot be found. In such a case one person can of course be able to embrace several objects of attachment at once, not only with the arms, but also with the soul, and it may be possible that a man, if he has a very large soul, must have recourse to a dozen or more women in order to fill it; yes, he may even feel sincere good-will towards each one of them, and may value each one especially for her individual qualities, just as we value the qualities of various flowers. But this can as little be an entirely satisfactory relation for each one of the twelve loved ones as for the man himself, if he is capable of a real, passionate, *i.e.*, a true, love, which cannot be otherwise than exclusive. He will, should he even have the choice among a thousand women, still feel a void, and gladly exchange the thousand for a single one whom he can love as his ideal with complete devotion.

---

* " Du füllest meine Seele ganz."

For common men, or men corrupted by our present education, it is a mere pretext for their inclinations towards the harem if they put up a doctrine of the "plurality of love;" uncorrupted men can at most look upon the doctrine as a make-shift for the misfortune of not having an opportunity in this perverse world for a free choice according to natural affinity. In a world as it ought to be the exclusiveness of love will be all the more a law because no free woman will want to share a beloved man with another, and *vice versa*.

Thus we have reached the subject of jealousy. I would not designate jealousy either as an "inborn" nor as an "inbred" passion. It is an accidental passion, for which the faculty indeed is inborn. In its nobler form and in its nobler motives it arises from love and can, according to circumstances and the character of the person from whom it emanates, differ in its nature and in its mode of expression. The noblest jealousy is a sort of ambition or pride of the loving person who feels it as an insult that another one should assume it as possible to supplant his love, or it is the highest degree of devotion which sees a desecration of its object in the foreign invasion, as it were, of his own altar. A jealousy of this sort, which would fain keep away everything unworthy from the beloved person, is far superior to that lower grade which arises from the anxiety of losing the beloved object through the approach of another, perhaps worthier, person. This sort of jealousy arises either from weakness, which from a sense of its own want of lovable qualities is not convinced of being sure of its cause, or from distrust, which perhaps, by applying its own standard inversely, thinks the beloved person capable of infidelity. Sometimes all these motives may act together.

The lowest species of jealousy is a sort of avarice or envy which, without being capable of love, at least wishes to possess the object of its jealousy alone by the one party assuming a sort of property right over the other. This jealousy, which might be called the Sultanic, is generally to be found with old withered "husbands" whom the devil has prompted to marry young women and who forthwith dream night and day of cuckold's horns. These Argus-eyed keepers are no longer capable of any feeling that could be called love, they are rather as a rule heartless house-tyrants ; at the same time they cannot, therefore, make their wife happy. But they grudge her every happy relationship, because their egotism will not allow them to admit their own incapacity by granting her a compensation, or because they wish to possess alone the very thing they do not deserve, in order to abuse it. They revenge their own want of amiability by deposing from office, so to speak, the (real or supposed) amiability of their wife. I have known a man who, loathed by

his wife like carrion, paid no other attention to her
than to watch her with restless anxiety and to
pursue her with querulous jealousy. She died
suddenly by an accident. Did the husband fall
into despair on account of her loss? God forbid!
The weight of a mountain was taken from him,
and he called out, relieved: "Now she cannot at
least belong to any one else!" So he himself did
not lose anything in her; still he could not bear
the thought that she should be possessed by another. That proves that jealousy does not come
from love alone.

The general conclusion will be that jealousy is
more the result of wrong conditions which cause
uncongenial unions and which through moral corruption artificially create distrust, than a necessary
accompaniment of love. Let us imagine a community consisting of ten, a hundred, a thousand
couples, all of them united by true love. Is jealousy possible among these two thousand lovers?
I do not think so, because every single individual
is sure of his or her beloved object through reciprocated love. Now let us imagine this community
expanded into an entire nation, educated according
to reason, in which both sexes have every possible
opportunity for making acquaintances and entering into suitable unions: jealousy will be banished
by the simple assurance of love.

The lady who asked the questions traced jealousy to self-esteem. At the same time she calls

attention to the fact that even animals are jealous. Do the animals then possess self-esteem? If I understood the questioner rightly, she meant to say that whoever esteemed himself could not bear to be neglected by the beloved person in favor of a third. But it seems to me that in such a case self-esteem would not dictate jealousy, but rather withdrawal from a relation in which the interest taken in a third person plainly shows us that we are no longer wanted.

Another lady-friend writes me that jealousy always made her indignant; either two persons were guaranteed to each other by love, and then there was no need of watching each other with Argus-eyes, or love did not exist, and then there ought to be a separation; should her husband torment her with jealousy, she would look at it as a want of confidence, as an insult, as a disparagement of herself.

I for my part can understand jealousy, but not, as it were, expound it. It is a passion with which precisely those are most afflicted who are the least worthy of love. An innocent maiden who enters marriage will not dream of getting jealous; but all her innocence cannot secure her against the jealousy of her husband if he has been a libertine. Those are wont to be the most jealous who have the consciousness that they themselves are most deserving of jealousy. Most men in consequence of their present education and corruption have so poor an opinion not only of the male but even of the female sex that they believe every woman at every moment capable of what they themselves have looked for among all and have found among the most unfortunate, the prostitutes.

When jealousy is justifiable, it generally is so among women. A woman whose early confidence has been shaken by special signs, and who is now tormented by constant anxiety, without attaining to any certainty about the infidelity of the man she loves, is in a position deserving deepest sympathy and no reproach. But she also is suffering from the perversity of conditions which make hypocrites of her husband and his accomplices.

The most objectionable thing about jealousy is that it attempts to fetter the person against whom it is directed, that it would deprive him of freedom of action, of the right of free control over himself. This despotism of jealousy is connected with marriage, as it has been hitherto, and with the legal inequality of the sexes. If the sexual union of two sovereign individuals is actually made into a relation of serfdom, it is but natural that especially the stronger party will presume to punish the emancipation of the other as a crime. Hence the brutality of vulgar husbands, who, after having in every possible and intolerable manner forfeited their wife's love, believe themselves justified in killing her when her precious lord has become revolting to her and another one pleases her better.   Such cases are especially adapted to enlighten us as to the nature and the consequences of common jealousy.   But whoever has reached those lofty heights of liberty and humanity where he will grant every individual the right of sovereignty over himself cannot wish to forcibly hold any one in a relation that does not conform to his wishes ; and even if it should come hard to him to see a beloved person, or one become indispensable by habit, make use of her right of sovereignty in favor of a third person, he would still silence his jealousy in consequence of his appreciation of the rights of others.   It can moreover be considered as having the force of a mathematical certainty that the party who voluntarily turns away from the other is so little suited to the other that the latter can anywhere find a substitute.

MORALITY.

PIETY has nothing else to oppose to immorality as it has been sketched in the preceding chapter than unnatural restraints and hypocrisy. Reason has no part in this senseless undertaking; she recognizes the claims of nature and its needs openly and frankly, but tries to regulate its manifestations by reasonable and truly moral conditions.

It is the task of mankind to follow nature under the guidance of reason. To depart from nature and to return to nature along the path or in the form of civilization is the evolutionary process of humanity and the humane spirit. Mere nature is coarseness or dependence; to reproduce, as it were, nature through reason, with consciousness—that is civilization and liberty.

Let us begin with liberty itself. The savage is free: but his natural freedom is subjugated in order to return at a later period as cultivated liberty come to consciousness of itself. Just so with morals. The natural relation of the sexes is lost in immorality and hypocrisy, in order to return as free love in moral consciousness and form. Natural liberty in the process of civilization passes through the school of slavery to true freedom, and natural morality through the school of immorality to true morality.

Civilization and liberty make man a moral being. To recognize the natural laws by means of reason, and to execute them freely for the purpose of, or within the limits of, civilization—that is moral destiny, moral endeavor, moral life. Man is by means of reason lord of his nature, not for the sake of suppressing it, but that he may, as it were, renew it as his handiwork in ennobled form.

Let us apply these principles of liberty and morality to natural needs. The animal is by nature limited in its desires; instinct directs it and binds it within definite tracks of needs, to step out of which it has neither the power nor the temptation. It does not eat in order to eat, or to enjoy itself by eating, but only to appease its hunger, and when it has eaten its fill it is also satisfied; it mates from a physical need in a definite measure and at definite times, and outside of these times the sexual instinct is of itself quiescent. Neither in appeasing its hunger nor in satisfying its sexual instinct can it impel itself beyond the measure fixed by nature, or, as it were, compose variations to the theme of nature. In a word, it is not free, but merely a slave of nature. Man, however, is free. To him no need is merely physically prescribed or measured out; he has rather the liberty than the instinct to overstep his mere need, to make the indulgence of it an "enjoyment" and to overdo the "enjoyment." Did he not have the liberty and the capacity to overstep the necessity of nature, neither would he have the liberty and the capacity to refrain from transgressing. That he refrains from reasonable motives, that he regulates his impulse in accordance with reasonable aims, that he through his reason shows his liberty the measure of its use, that he consciously and voluntarily fulfils the aim of nature as the animal does unconsciously and involuntarily—that is his pride, that is morality.

To deny nature or to thwart the aims of nature, which in a manner furnish reason with the material for morality, can never be moral ; it is rather just as immoral as on the other side a transgression of the natural limits and objects. An old maid (who purposely renounces her sexual nature) is therefore just as immoral as a courtesan, and a celibate just as immoral as a libertine.

The false ideas of morality with respect to sexual affairs show themselves in what we commonly call the sense of shame.

What is the sense of shame ? Generally speaking, it is the diffidence about exposing something, or the pain at having exposed something which may meet with the disapproval of others. Without this respect for others there would be no sense of shame. The existence or the degree of shame, therefore, directly depends on the conception of the one feeling ashamed, and this conception depends on the real or supposed opinion of others towards whom this sense of shame shows itself. But the correctness or falseness of this opinion determines whether there is any occasion for shame or not.

If we think of mankind in a state of nature, we can hardly suppose that such a thing as sexual shame existed between man and woman. But if we follow up the progress of development the growth of shame can easily be explained from externals. The periodic indisposition of woman gradually began to impress the man disagreeably: the woman concealed it—she was ashamed. Pregnancy with its consequences disfigured feminine beauty: the woman draped herself—she was ashamed. In the course of propagation deformities and cripples arose: the deformed woman improved her shape with artificial means—she was ashamed. Children born outside of marriage, who were not supported by any *pater familias*, and whom the mother could not support, became the burden of others ; pregnancy outside of marriage was therefore condemned : the woman made a secret of it—she was ashamed. The excesses of certain shameless periods brought about reactions which, with the immoderate practice, likewise condemned the moderate practice; therefore all sexual manifestations had to be avoided : people were ashamed. And since religion has even pressed the stamp of holiness on every suppression of nature,

intimidated nature has become entirely shame-
faced, and all the world is ashamed. But with
regard to the very things on account of which it
ought to be most ashamed it has become totally
shameless.

There is therefore no absolute sense of shame,
and the present sense of shame in sexual matters
is not a spontaneous emotion rooted in nature and
continuous with it, but, as above stated, dependent on the judgment of others and a product of
circumstances.*

If we measure the sense of shame by the standard of reason, it is justifiable only when it con-
forms to true morality, and is therefore the *expression of the moral consciousness*, and in this way
we come to understand that the preachers of
shame are sometimes the true preachers of immorality, of that immorality which would further
morality by the suppression of nature and truth.
It is surely not at all necessary to go about naked
in order to show that one is free from false shame,
nor is it necessary to love each other on the public thoroughfare in order to prove that one recognizes the claims of nature; but only a fool or a
hypocrite will want to sacrifice the inner law to
external considerations, and incorruptible nature
to ridiculous prejudices.

---

* Compare the festival of Priapus with Christian hypocrisy,
and then ask wherein the essence of shame consists.

Let us meet the hypocrites with straightforward language.

Is it immoral that the breast of the youth and the maiden is filled with the longing of love? No! Why then do you, priests, demand that they should be ashamed of it, when they have not asked your permission? *You* are the immoral ones.

Is it immoral that a woman should bear a child to her beloved? No! Why do you cast her out, then? You are the immoral ones, the barbarians. You will demand that the trees shall be ashamed to blossom and to bear fruit.

The human being who is ashamed of his nature is not worthy to be a human being. What reasonable ground can you preachers of morality find for shame which you, under the conditions which you have decreed, connect with sexual love and the act which causes the existence of man? You might with the same right subject eating and drinking to your conditions and expose them to condemnation. If you are ashamed of the sentiment and the act which caused your existence, you ought also to be ashamed of your existence itself, for which you sometimes have sufficient reason.

There is no greater and more senseless barbarity than that "moral" passion for condemning which makes the pregnancy of woman a disgrace if nature has not been granted permission by priest or justice of the peace to increase the race. The pregnant woman should under all conditions be "sacred," should stand under the protection and receive the sympathy of the entire community which she is about to increase with an at *all* events innocent member. Instead of that, it is made out a crime that she has found opportunity, without the aid of the justice of the peace or the priest, to present the community with a new member, and the hatred and persecution of ignorance is incited against the unfortunate one, as if the intention actually were to make a suicide or an infanticide of her. Recently a poor woman hanged herself in Switzerland because she believed herself pregnant and her neighbors shared this belief and made her the target of their respectable vituperations and "moral" persecutions. When the suicide was examined, her pregnancy proved to have been only imagined! She died as a victim of nature-disdaining vulgarity, and her murderers were the pious, moralizing clergy. The corpses of unfortunate women which you take from the water, the remains of murdered children which you find in sewers, the bodies of despairing mothers whom you drag to the gallows —these are the witnesses of your pious humanity that builds prisons instead of lying-in hospitals, and that would have hell make foundling-houses superfluous. In Paris foundlings are taken care of as "*enfants de la patrie;*" in New York, **for** instance, the "*enfants de la patrie*" are deposited in the gutters of the street. The rich seduce the girls, the priests curse the seduced girls, and the seduced girls murder the sharers of their poverty and the proofs of their imaginary shame. This is in three words the morality of our present hypocritical society in these matters.

When you have wedded your daughters to rich *roués*, you welcome their children with joy; if your family is increased by a poor lover, who is not able to "marry," then you heap reproaches on the mother. The reason for the disgrace which you create does not lie therefore in the act to which you try to attach it, but in the single miserable circumstance that *you must support the children of your daughters*. But if this is the reason of your anger, then why not have the courage to call it by its right name, and do not commit the hypocrisy of expressing a pecuniary consideration in the form of a condemnation of human nature in its most beautiful impulse. You will then reach the conclusion that it is not love that is to blame, but the unnatural conditions which hinder thousands, yes, millions, from living out their natural instincts in a moral relation.

How must a Héloïse, who, although surrounded by the piety of the Middle Ages, would rather be the lover than the legal wife of Abèlard—how must she appear to you, coarse fellows, who judge love only from the standpoint of priests, and mother hood from that of the shopkeeper! She was a great woman, one of the greatest women of history; and you, according to your ideas, you must classify her with the " immoral," because you are not human beings, but priests.

If you want to cultivate shame, then base it upon the strictest ideas of true morality; but do not look for this morality in the domain of your conventional stupidity, your inhuman unnaturalness, and your shameful hypocrisy.

It is not immoral if a man and a woman, even "*unmarried*," give themselves up to true love; but it is immoral if an old *roué* marries a young girl whom he knowingly cannot make happy, merely for her physical charms.

It is not immoral if a man and a woman, even " unmarried," give themselves up to true love; but it is immoral if the man merely uses the woman for the satisfaction of his lust, without giving dignity to the relation by real affection or taking his share of the responsibility in the fate of the loving one.

It is not immoral if a woman unites herself with the man whom she loves against the wish of another; but it is immoral if she becomes the wife of a man whom she does not love, because another wishes it.*

---

* How far "morality" can go astray in such cases where personal liberty and free inclination submit to a "higher will ' is shown among other things in the " New Héloïse " by Rou≈

It is not immoral to get tired of a legal husband upon closer acquaintance and to conceive a new love for another man ; but it is immoral to continue, or to be obliged to continue, the old relation notwithstanding this new love.

It is not immoral to consider " chastity " in itself just as much of a stupidity as starvation in itself ; but it is immoral to carry " unchastity " to the point of excess.

It is not immoral to persuade a woman to yield herself, but it is immoral to offer her nothing as the prize of her devotion but a feigned love.

In short, it is immoral to disregard the equal rights of the other sex ; to abuse it for selfish ends ; to falsify or to confuse the ends of nature ; to degrade the sexual relation simply to a means for frivolously satisfying the senses or for low speculations ; to disfigure the beauty of sexual love by priestly nonsense; to pollute true sentiment by coarse hypocrisy. Be ashamed of *these* immoralities *and you will no longer need any other shame !*

There is, indeed, another kind of shame, which ought, however, not to bear this name, since no moral flavor attaches to it. It is that delicate shyness which the virgin feels when she is to step be-

---

seau. Her chief virtue consisted in the disgusting and unpoetic immorality of marrying a man entirely indifferent to her from filial "duty," and of generating children with him under the very eyes of her lover, whom she sacrifices to "duty." Shame on this " moral " prostitution!

yond the boundary of virginity, as well as that feminine reserve which strives to hide or to guard her charms. This "shame" is either a natural consequence of an emotional affection upon entering a new life, or it is the expression of an unconscious policy in love that is chary with its charms in order not to depreciate or to profane them. Or it may also be the unconscious expression of a feeling which tells a woman that nature has not given her the initiative of love. Finally, it may be the expression of modesty which fears that she cannot come up to the high expectations which the enthusiastic man has of the charms of his beloved.

This "shame," which has nothing to do with the consciousness or the fear of seeing something improper disclosed, is an ornament to every woman, and its absence is a proof of dulness and coarseness.

MARRIAGE.

Is marriage a relation which is or can be imposed by the State, by religion, by the police, by
the clergy, by relatives, or by any other power?

Everybody will answer: It is the union of a
man and a woman resulting from spontaneous affection.   Therefore only each particular couple
that enters into such a union carries the motive
and the aim of the union within itself, and no
power in the world has the right to control this
motive or to stipulate what the aim shall be.
Only liberty in entering into and liberty in dissolving marriage can secure its character, determine its moral nature, and guarantee the attainment of its end.

The chief end of marriage can be expressed in
three words: Propagation, Love, Friendship.

We have seen in the chapter on Morality in
what respect man differs from the animal in the
gratification of his natural needs.   This difference
refers not only to the gratification of the sexual
need, but also to its consequences: propagation.
The animal propagates unconsciously, and sepa-
rates itself from its young just as unconsciously
as soon as they are able to provide their own

food. And even this unconscious care emanates chiefly only from the mother, while the male generally concerns himself neither for the mother nor the young after copulation. The well-known passionate love of animals for their young is at an end from the time when the latter no longer need aid, and old and young no longer know each other.

The egotism and coarse conception of men would fain have transferred this mode of propagation also to the human race. That would mean in other words: we want to be animals in this respect, not human beings. While the animal sees in the female only an instrument for procreation, the woman is to the man only the complement of his being, his second ego, in and with whom he begins to live his complete life ; while in the animal a merely temporary affection secures the indispensable aid for the rearing of the young, children are to men a desirable continuation of their own personality through whom they establish their continuity beyond death with the infinite stream of humanity. And through this ethical continuity and the ethical consequences of sexual intermingling there arises between man and woman, between father and mother, between parents and children, that relation which we designate by the word *family*.

Thus with regard to propagation, family life at once makes an essential distinction between man and the animal. To want to destroy the family is either a great error or a great vulgarity. It is founded in nature, and when viewed in the light of its ethical import it lays the foundation of the most beautiful, the truest, and the surest human happiness. The animal has no family because it has no reason ; reason cannot desire to destroy the family, because it would thereby only re-establish crude nature, that is, destroy morality and, with morality, itself.

But the more the importance of the family is appreciated by society and by the individual, the higher and nobler the conception of it is, the more must its fundamental condition be recognized as that liberty which alone admits of complete harmony, of true attachment, of sincere union between man and woman. Nothing must be allowed to influence the choice except spontaneous affection ; nothing must stand in the way of a separation where this affection, and with it the desire of a union, is wanting. The family is inconceivable without real marriage, marriage is inconceivable without love, and love can no longer be distinguished from prostitution when the free bond of the union is vitiated by compulsion. If propagation, to return to this point, is to have an ethical significance and ethical consequences, it must not proceed on the plane of bestial association, but just as little in false or forced relationships. Every child that springs from a union which would have ceased had not external considerations or binding fetters held it together, transmits the curse of the misfortune and of the immorality to the next generation.

As a second end of marriage, which we must at the same time call its origin, I designate love. I shall spare myself the trouble of combating those philosophers who would deny the existence of love. At the same time I do not content my-self with conceiving of love only in its romantic form, and I do not care to construct a corner-stone of the moral order of things from an intox-ication of the senses or of the imagination. I shall let the happiness which accompanies this in-toxication stand in all its beauty wherever it is present ; but we must place its substance on a basis of reason, and make a consciousness of the intox-ication. This is accomplished by tracing love to man's perfect consciousness of his sovereignty in the world, of his worth and his liberty, and then, moreover, to the true recognition of the advan-tages of external and internal beauty which satisfy not only a sensual but, at the same time, an ethical and æsthetical need in the lovers. Lovers must come to be to each other that which men have hitherto placed above the clouds by the words "god" and "goddess;" yes, they must become even more to each other, namely, the realized ideal of their moral conceptions and of their sense of beauty. If they learn to seek and to appreciate each other in this sense, love will become a lasting enthusiasm, and the words of Schiller, which unfortunately apply to most of our present relationships, will have become untrue:

> With that sweetest holiday
> Must the May of life depart ;
> With the cestus loosed—away
> Flies illusion from the heart.*

On the contrary, the illusion will become a beautiful truth. Every real love of noble, intelligent people will only be confirmed by sexual union. The so-called " nuptial bed " is the grave of false, but the ark of covenant of true, love.

The want of love always consists either in moral degeneration or in a wrong choice. Let men be educated for love, and leave to them the liberty to annul a wrong choice by separation, and true marriage will crowd out a thousand relationships which now are nothing but institutions for the perpetuation of misery and prostitution.

Love is called "blind." To what purpose? Supposing it could be demonstrated that the passionate attachment of two people was an illusion which augmented and beautified their respective qualities, the happiness which they would mutually prepare for each other would not therefore

---

* Ach ! des Lebens schönste Feier
Endigt auch den Lebensmai ;
Wit dem Gürtel, mit dem Schleier
Reisst der schöne Wahn entzwei.

be destroyed. But by their conception of each
other they at all events show their ability to
form a certain ideal ; and if in the course of their
acquaintance it becomes apparent that they have
not reached this ideal, their experience may serve
as a guide which will enable them to find it all
the surer in another relationship.

As for the rest, many an argument might be
brought forward against the blindness of love. I
should be much inclined to credit it with clear-
sightedness. The loving interest sharpens the
vision for the detection and appreciation of qualities which the indifferent person would overlook
or fail to appreciate. Thus above all those are
blind who charge love with blindness, and it is
only necessary to view men from the standpoint
of love in order to secure to them the recognition
and appreciation of their qualities.

But the question will be raised : Will love, after
all these concessions are made to it, be sufficient
to fill out an entire life? Can it, even if it out-
lasts the honeymoon and the time which might
suffice to test the possibility of an illusion,—can it
satisfy the heart so long that its value will not be
lost in the need for change which would finally
lead to an anarchy of the affections ?

This question brings us to the third word with
which I designated the end and substance of marriage—to friendship.

Of course I hold that love in marriage changes

from a state of passionate attachment into a condition of quiet friendship; but at the same time,
I maintain that true friendship exists only in marriage.

The question whether between persons of the
same sex real friendship is possible has never, so
far as I know, been met with a doubt. And yet
I am very much inclined to answer it with a down-
right no.

All sympathies and antipathies of men are
founded in egoism in the good sense. Self-interest is the natural guide in all steps, and there is
no danger in acknowledging this when a correct,
general principle is added to this guide as its test,
that is, when the pursuit of self-interest is placed
under moral control.

The duration and value of a union between two
people depends entirely on whether these persons
are fitted to conform to their respective egoisms,
that is, to mutually satisfy their needs, be these
needs intellectual, emotional, or physical. But
now it is clear, and experience confirms it every
day, that two persons of the same sex, even if in
individual qualities they attract or agree with each
other, can yet never in the long-run have in all
things the same interests, but will sooner or later
in some case or other show themselves as competitors. Individual examples to the contrary occur
only where exaggeration and exaltation sacrifice
the personal interests of the different persons to

an abstraction of friendship, or where circumstances keep both persons at a certain distance from each other, so that the competition of the respective interests finds no point of conflict. If a conflict and an estrangement are to be avoided in a constant living together, one person must so far give up his independence that the preponderance of the other changes into domineering guidance. But if this is the case, the true conception of the friendship which is to exist between persons of the same sex is lost.

Among men it is now ambition, now partisanship, now the friction of character, now a difference in principles, etc.; among women it is generally competition in love, jealousy, vanity, etc., which causes the rupture of friendships. (Examples of friendship among women are hardly ever to be found except with old maids who have resigned all human impulses, especially sexual competition.) But these points of collision disappear entirely by the side of the all-conclusive fact that persons of the same sex do not at all possess, and *cannot* possess, the qualities which enable them to satisfy each other entirely, to complement each other entirely, and, I might say, to let the cogs of their egoism work exactly into each other. *The man can never fill the place of a woman to the man, the woman can never fill that of a man to the woman, but the man can fill the place of a woman to the woman, and the woman the place of a man to the man.* The inadequacy of friendship among persons of the same sex the Greeks have shown most strikingly in their attempt to complete, as it were, the friendships into which the abnormal taste of the times had led the men by the unnatural introduction of the feminine element of "love." Accustomed to look upon women as inferior beings, but not able to withdraw themselves entirely from the acknowledgment of the feminine element, they transferred it, as it seems, partly to youths in order to sanction its acknowledgment through the male sex. And while thereby unconsciously degrading woman, they avenged her at the same time in themselves, by their endeavor to complete, to idealize themselves by the feminine element.

The two sexes are designed to complement each other, to perfect the human being in each. This completion is the bond of true friendship; and if, on the one hand, the writer is not entirely wrong who says, " One man and one woman are together equal to two angels, two women are together equal to two devils;" Rousseau, on the other hand, hits the truth exactly when he says, " A man's best friend is his wife." I admit that the psychological interest and common ideal aims can bring about a relationship between men which deserves the name of friendship ; but, according to our views, perfect friendship demands complete devotion, complete confidence, and mutual indispensableness, which exists as little among men as among women, and is only conditioned by a difference of sex.

Also with regard to the external development of character the difference of the two sexes is very well adapted to establish a relation of friendship. While the man as the representative of strength impresses the woman, the clinging nature of woman seems made for the purpose of subordinating herself to the male predominance without losing her personality or lapsing into servile dependence. On the other hand, man will make concessions to the weak woman which he would never make to a rival in strength. Only man and woman can unite a proper subordination with a just coördination in a natural way.

But woman is not only clinging, she is also faithful, sincere, and sacrificing. The woman grows into the relation with her friend with her whole soul ; and where the uncouth egoism or the polemical nature of the man would allow a break to appear, the love of the woman knows at once how to mend it. The woman is the uniting element in the formation, and the conciliatory element in the preservation, of the relationship. The woman is not only a perfect friend, she even does not cease to be one unless the man makes the friendship altogether impossible. If I must bethink myself whether I have ever had perfect friends among men, I am on the other hand quite certain that I have found perfect friends among women.

Since we are here speaking of marriage, it is self-evident that friendship can be understood only as one of the forms or modifications of love. It is love without the passion of love ; it is love without sensuality ; it is benevolence, confidence, and attachment ushered in and confirmed by sexual devotion and union.   It combines, therefore, I might say, at the same time the greatest absence of egoism with the satisfaction of egoism, and is thus perfectly adapted to establish a relationship for the whole life.   It is not to be inferred from this, however, that a true marriage necessarily can only exist in a union for life.

Having established the three chief aims and requirements of marriage, we have still to refute one point that refers to a peculiar right which men claim to possess over women—a right which, if it did exist, would make every marriage impossible.   I mean the pretended right of sensual extravagance.

We have seen the degeneracy of the male sex with regard to love.   Woman has remained the vestal who has preserved the fire of love in its purity, while man has smothered it in the smoke of sensual passion.   While man in general is always sensually disposed, even without feeling the least higher interest for the woman who serves him, the passion of woman is generally awakened only by love; and giving herself up without attachment is entirely foreign to the true and noble woman. With her, the passion does not attach merely to the sex as with man, but at the same time to the person. Excellent women have without reserve told me their thoughts on this point. They admit the possibility that in an unguarded moment even a stranger, by an impressive beauty and manliness, could place the woman in a state of sensual excitement, but that she would still be far from yielding to this excitement even in such a case, and that in any case the relation could not be at an end for the woman and her wish fulfilled by mere physical yielding. This was not a mere matter of education, but had its foundation in the nature of woman.

Woman is sensual when she loves, while man, as a rule, loves only when he is sensual. The question now is simply this: Is there an essential difference of nature or not? Is there a peculiar need for sensuality in man aside from love, and, therefore, a peculiar right for him, or not? Or can it be demanded of him that he should, like woman, *restrain his sensuality within the limits of love?* There are points to be considered here upon which a great deal depends, but on which no settled views seem as yet to have been developed, mainly for the reason that either hypocrisy or egotism would not lay them open for discussion. I, however, have made up my mind to discuss all human questions in a human manner. Only vulgarity and a bad conscience can fear being led too far in such a discussion.

The general opinion amounts to this, that the man has greater sensual needs, especially a greater need for change, therefore also a greater right to satisfy it than the woman. I have even heard intellectual men who were not by education especially disposed towards sensuality, and who in every way distinguished themselves by moral aspirations, express themselves to the effect that in the society of the future man could not be restricted to a single woman, but would have to be granted the liberty of living with a certain number of women—who, however, need not live together—in a simultaneous marriage relation.

So the man is to be a sort of human rooster, as it were, who keeps a court of human hens.

If women were hens, it is not at all to be doubted that the roosters would assemble in sufficient numbers about them. But the first difficulty with which we meet here is the *opposition of the women.* If we inquire among all women, not a single one will be found who would be willing to share a beloved man with another woman, except she had been deprived of her reason by a silly fanaticism, as is the case with the Mormons. The Count of Gleichen would in our time have to narrow down his broad nuptial couch to one half its dimensions. Only very superior and imposing manly personalities, as for instance Goethe, have succeeded in making several women at the same time *partially* happy, or in silencing in them the opposition of rivalry, which by no means is equivalent to assent. Woman is guided by the proper feeling that a *real marriage relation can exist only between two persons.* And if the woman, in accordance with this feeling, resents the proposal to share her lover with other women, she only makes use of her *right ;* and in formulating this right she will ask men this question : *Which one of you would be willing to be required to share his beloved with other men ?*

Whatever a man or a woman possesses of love, confidence, and devotion can be entirely bestowed upon *one* person. It is impossible to simultaneously love two men or two women truly. A man can have twenty mistresses at the same time, but not two wives. But woman has a right to be a *wife*, she has a right to demand that everything should be given her which she herself offers, and it is to misunderstand her right, no less than the nature of marriage, when one expects a woman to be content to lie in wait, as it were, with her love, till her lover has made the round among colleagues, and her turn for a visit has come.

Woman does not ask for several men, but one she wishes to possess wholly. Only degenerate women, inured to immorality by education and surroundings, or prompted by an abnormal physical constitution, can entertain relations with several men at the same time, or even follow the footsteps of a Messalina, of whom Juvenal says that she was wont to return home from the haunts of lust "worn out but not satisfied." If, on the ground of their sensual capacity, men would establish a right to have "conjugal relations" with several women at the same time, they have an opportunity to become convinced by Parisian Messalinas that women could insist on the right to have fifty husbands, where a man would ask but for five wives.

But, on the other hand, they could be convinced by the example of noble women who have given themselves up to love in full freedom without regard for the judgment of the world, that it is not a need of the feminine sex to have several men at their disposal *at the same time.* Ninon, George Sand, and others have not been content with one love relation, but they have never loved two men at the same time ; *i.e.,* they have never stood in conjugal relations with two men at once. They kept every relationship pure until it had outlived itself, and then entered into a new one, *i.e.,* into a new marriage. And they would surely have confined themselves to a single man, had they found one who had possessed the qualities that could have interested such extraordinary women and made them happy for life.

We can, therefore, consider it as an established fact that the woman, just as she does not crave several husbands at the same time, will also not tolerate a rival in the marriage relation. Could it, therefore, be doubtful whether a man must restrict himself to one wife at a time, woman would be the one to decide. It would be contrary to reason to assume that the nature of man required several women at the same time, while it was the nature of woman, on the other hand, to treat the removal of this need as a vital question. Where there have been or still are nations among whom the husband, beside his legal wife, kept concubines (for instance among savages, the ancients, and Mussulmen), there we find this abuse founded upon the disqualification and degradation of woman, who will submit to it only so long as she has not attained to a consciousness of herself. Such a degradation has the same origin as that of the women of India, who are obliged to throw themselves into the flames in honor of their dead husbands. I come to the conclusion, therefore, that the claims of men to variety are founded entirely upon past conditions and past education, and that woman will have to recall them within the proper limits. The man who, on the plane of our civilization, desires several wives at the same time comes, therefore,

1) into opposition with the will of each one of them, and can attain his end only through deceit and concealment ;

2) he violates justice ;

3) he offends the dignity of woman ; and,

4) he destroys marriage, and with it the moral element in the relation of the sexes.

How, then, secure marriage and morality? How remove the objection of male desire, which under present conditions is always striving to overstep the boundaries of morality?

The attainment of this end cannot be hoped for, after all that has hitherto been considered, without fulfilling the following requirements:

1) Guarding youth from secret vices by careful education, adequate occupation, and close attention, so that the lustful instinct may not be cultivated abnormally early, and undermine the capacity for sexual love.

2) Early marriage of youths and maidens, in order that the want of opportunity to satisfy the awakened sexual needs may not drive them into wrong ways. It is here to be observed that the premature development of sexual desire is nothing but the consequence of our bad education hitherto, and that the young man has no sexual needs to satisfy previous to his marriage. Thus he is, on entering marriage, not yet addicted to licentiousness, his first sexual gratification coincides with his first love, and thus he is led back to the plane of morality on which that portion of the feminine sex which has not fallen a prey to prostitution has remained. *The gratification of the sexual instinct is thus wholly placed within the*

marriage relation. But in order that it become possible to uphold this moral barrier, we must

3) not restrict the liberty of marriage by tedious formalities and impeding conditions. The agreement of the lovers and a notice concerning their union must suffice for the forming of marriage. The priest does not make marriage, the law does not make marriage, the parents do not make marriage, the magistrate does not make marriage, but love and the agreement of the lovers make it. Let marriage, therefore, be made dependent on nothing save the conditions for its existence.

4) The liberty which prevails in the contracting of marriage must also prevail in the dissolution of marriage. Whether the object of marriage has been attained can only be decided by the judgment of those who have contracted it. If they do not feel satisfied, to attempt to preserve it by force means to destroy it by force. By this force the very thing would again be introduced which is chiefly to be prevented, namely, dissipation outside of marriage. *The married do not exist for the sake of marriage, but marriage exists for the sake of the married.* The bond must, therefore, be severed when it has become a fetter. What is the object of marriage? As we have seen: propagation, love, friendship. And to this you want to force us by making separation *more difficult?* Strange lunacy!

5) State education of the children. When pa-

rents are fettered to the marriage relation longer than perhaps during the first years, by the care for the support and education of the children, there arises, especially in disordered economic conditions, either the danger that they will fulfil their paternal duties at the price of marriage by remaining together contrary to their inclinations, or that, in case of a separation, the burden of supporting the children will fall on one party only, or, finally, that this support will turn out to the disadvantage of the children. If the parents have sufficient means to dispense with the assistance of the State, they will of course, even without it, be secured against the danger of sacrificing their love or their liberty to their cares; but most of them are without means, and the State certainly loses nothing if by bearing the cost of education it buys of them the opportunity to rear moral and happy citizens instead of immoral and unhappy ones. So long, however, as the State has not reached the point where, as a last resort, it secures an education to all children, it is self-evident that with the liberty to dissolve marriage *ad libitum* must remain the common obligation of the parents to take upon themselves the education and support of their children.

The objections and doubts which will be raised against these requirements are easily to be foreseen, especially since, in judging of the prerequisites of a future development of social condi

tions, the opponent is but too ready to take existing conditions as a foundation for his suppositions. In the first place, a "moral" solicitude
will be expressed that the liberty of forming or
dissolving a marriage relation at pleasure will involve people in the danger of using marriage
merely as a means for variety in the satisfaction
of their desires. Unions will be made to-day
and unmade to-morrow, etc. Granted that such
a supposition could come true, we need only ask
ourselves the question whether the moral condition of society could thus become worse than it
now is. As if the present society could run any
sort of risk thereby! Could men be brought to a
higher and more disgusting degree of moral corruption than the present secret prostitution has
reached, even if freedom of lust should be publicly proclaimed? Certainly not. But let us take
another point of view. Let us picture to ourselves
a society consisting throughout of cultured, nor-
mally constituted people who have been educated
for liberty, and who feel themselves secure in their
chief interests, and let us ask ourselves whether in
such a society a man would value less the joys of
a sincere relation with a beloved woman, and the
happiness of seeing the continuance of his existence secured, as it were, in his children, than the
Turkish satisfaction of sleeping with a different
concubine every night. And let us, moreover,
keep in mind that the women of the future are not

the women of the present, and let us ask ourselves
whether they, when they have become economically independent of men, will still consent to, and
find their happiness in, being merely the changing
concubines of modern Turks. Those married people who are entirely suited to each other and are
happy together will certainly not separate for the
mere reason that they have full liberty to do so,
and those who are not happy together can by an
unrestricted change certainly not harm society as
much as they now do. Let us even consider the
possibility that a man might unite himself with a
different woman every year, and consider whether
it would be more immoral for him to have had a
dozen wives or several hundred mistresses during
his lifetime.

A further question by the doubters, who draw
their conclusion only from present conditions,
will be whether the liberty of changing the marriage relation, and the support of the children
by the State, would not have to result in the destruction of the family.

The family is formed by the mutual attachment
of the married couple, and by their love for their
children. This attachment and this love are a
natural need, and satisfy an interest than which
there is none higher and greater. It is, therefore,
an entirely false supposition that parents who
really love each other could find it to their inter-

est to dissolve the family; but for those who do not love each other the family has lost all value and all moral import. It is, therefore, a service to moral society to make dissolution possible to such families. Moreover, the need of parents to have their children constantly about them generally exists only during the early years of the latter. Finally, the admission of the children into public institutions does *not at all imply* their separation from the parents; the intercourse between them must rather always be left free to as large an extent as the purpose of the institution will permit.

It is self-evident that there ought not to exist any compulsion for the parents to give their children over to public institutions at a certain age; the State is only to offer the possibility and the opportunity for it. But if that is done in the right manner, it will appear that no compulsion is necessary.

No reasonable person will imagine that he can reach his ideal, whatever it may be. In all efforts at reform, the correct principle must be discovered and established as an ideal aim. The nearest possible approach is then a matter of circumstances and of practical possibilities. It is not to be expected, therefore, that the realization of the above requirements will eliminate all immoral elements from society. Neither can there be the least idea of creating a new state of things in a day, or of suddenly destroying the after-effects of former conditions. It is sufficient if the established principles are recognized as correct, gain adherents, and, as far as it is possible, serve the enlightened minds of both sexes even now as a guide for their actions.

ADULTERY.

ADHERENTS of the official and theological morality will feel in duty bound to grow indignant over the claim that in reality there is no such thing as adultery. They will believe that the moral world, whose chief aim hitherto seems to have been to create as many crimes as possible, in order to be able to condemn as much as possible, must go to ruin if it is deprived of one of its most piquant crimes. And nevertheless the world will finally have to submit to this loss, and even come to realize that in principle a more severe moral conception is required for the destruction of a piquant crime than for the retention of the same.

If there is to be a breach of marriage, the breach must necessarily extend through that which constitutes marriage, which is its essence, its condition, its sum and substance. Marriage is not a business contract, it is a union of hearts: and love is the condition of this union. A breach of marriage must, therefore, be a breach of love ; but love does not break itself ; its breaking is, therefore, equivalent to a want of love ; and since marriage without love is no longer marriage, so-called adultery can be nothing more than an actual proof that marriage no longer exists.

There can no more be a breach of marriage by adultery than there can be a breach of night, a breach of day, etc. When day dawns it is no longer night ; and when night comes it is no longer day. If one of the parties feels an inclination to commit what is called adultery, then the marriage is already broken, even without the completed act. At that very moment marriage ceases to exist, because love has ceased to exist ; because the love that is required for marriage either never existed or has been replaced by another.

Pious moralists will say that this is equivalent to giving free rein to adultery under the pretext of the dying out of the old and the awakening of a new love. But then these pious people do not know what love is. Love is no arbitrary thing. He who loves will and can as little abandon his love for any purpose as he who does not love can enforce a love for any purpose.

This is the very "moral" perversion of our moral ideas that has until now made it possible to bring in vogue and to maintain a style of marriage without the one requisite of marriage, love. True morality demands that a marriage which has ceased to be a marriage intrinsically, and which is, therefore, nothing more than a relation of compulsion, hypocrisy, and prostitution, should also cease to be one extrinsically. The hypocrisy of the pious moralists, however, still clings with all its might to the external relation, even after the purpose, the essence, and the contents have been lost and the inner bond has been rent in twain, and if one party withdraws from this compulsion in order to avenge outraged liberty outside of marriage, and to bring to light the fruits of enforced hypocrisy, this proof of a no longer existing marriage is called adultery.

Adultery is said to be a breach of faith. But what is faith? It is nothing more than active love. But if love is to be active, it must above all things exist. So long as I love I cannot become " unfaithful;" and as soon as I become unfaithful I no longer love. To assume fidelity as distinct from love is indeed a contradiction in the premises. Fidelity is love persisting in action and through action. It is, therefore, at bottom not at all a duty, but a frame of mind, or the necessary outcome of this frame of mind. Fidelity without this frame of mind, *i.e.*, merely physical or mechanical abstinence, cannot have the least moral value with regard to the essence and aim of marriage.

But it is again the men and the pious people who have made the discovery that there is also fidelity without love, without faithful sentiments, *i.e.*, self-denial which, for the sake of a foreign imaginary aim, must sacrifice its feelings to a false relationship. As we have seen above, man as the stronger had accustomed him self to use and abuse, by wilful change and in every manner, the degraded

weaker sex, in whom his coarse heart could not yet
find a lasting charm.   Still his feeling must gradually have brought him to reflect whether woman
had not really a right, and all the more a right, to
follow his example the oftener he set her that example.   Woman, however, made no use of this
right, because she continued ever to love him in
spite of his arbitrariness, and this undeserved fidelity appeared to him so astonishing and difficult that
he saw in it an exceptional virtue.   And since he
was an egotist and a despot, he came to claim this
fidelity which in the beginning had excited his
astonishment ; he came to demand fidelity of the
woman even when she no longer loved him, and
made a crime of unfaithfulness.   We have also
seen that among all savage peoples there is such
a thing as adultery on the part of woman, but not
on the part of man.   And even among civilized
nations the law makes an essential distinction.
Thus adultery on the part of woman is universally
a ground for divorce, but adultery on the part of
man generally only in such cases where the husband has kept a concubine in the common dwell-
ing.

When a woman becomes unfaithful her love has
also ceased.   No man will contest that.   His own
love, however, he wishes to be considered as independent of his fidelity, for he is as much a sophist
as a despot.   Goethe comforts one of his beloved
with the words :

Heart-felt love (!) unites us forever, and faithful (!) yearnings;
But desire (!) still craves the pleasures of change.(!)*

Indeed, "faithful love" by the side of "changing desires"! Interesting phenomenon! In other
words that would be : The respectability of our
existing relationship, and some of your amiable
qualities, move me from time to time to come
back to you from my excursions into other fields;
if I again tired of you I renew my excursions,
i.e., I take for myself full liberty to junket about
wherever I can find anything. You can be assured,
my dearest, that upon my excursions I never talk
the least about "love" to any other woman; no,
indeed not. I speak to her only of "desire." You
will be convinced, my child, that my junketing
can be charged only to "desire," which you
must by no means ever mistake for "love."
My "love" belongs to you alone, my "desire"
also to others, while others are satisfied with the
mere "desire" without "love," which you of
course will not be able to understand, but which
is nevertheless a lie. You can see from this, my
child, how beautifully we men can reconcile "fidelity" with "change" by separating love from fidelity, and either make the beloved one believe that
her competitors are mere mistresses or convince
her that she herself is one likewise ! We, however,

* Herzliche Liebe verbindet uns stets und treues Verlangen,
Nur den Wechsel behielt still die Begierde sich vor.

protest against the same liberty and science on your part in the name of all the principles of morality !

Goethe, to be sure, did not express this last sentence in words; but neither this liberal friend of women nor any other one would have declared himself contented if his beloved had surprised him with the news :

> Heart-felt love unites us forever and faithful yearnings;
> But desire still craves the pleasures of change.

Let us meet in advance an objection which will be raised against the theory of adultery as here set forth. On the basis of the old conceptions it will be said that this theory would logically protect and argue away every violation of duty. But the very end to be sought is the release of the essence and conditions of marriage from the bonds of duty in which it has been chained, and to place it unfettered upon the ground upon which it thrives—upon the ground of spontaneous attachment. The present moralists acknowledge marriages in which the sense of duty takes the place of attachment or makes it unnecessary; a sense of duty, namely, which is stimulated or dictated by external considerations. But true liberty and morality cannot acknowledge such marriages, for they are thoroughly immoral. A duty can never exist at the expense of ethical conceptions and ethical aims. But what is the aim of marriage? As we have seen: propagation, love, friendship. And who will and can impose that as a duty if our own free inclination does not prompt us to it? There are, indeed, duties in marriage, but they do not belong here, because in a true marriage they are recognized and practised spontaneously. With regard to adultery, they could at most consist in the avoidance of a possible danger into which at last every relationship may drift. To rashly expose the affections to every danger, or to wilfully put them to the test, would be to degrade them beforehand. Who would throw the crystal upon the pavement simply to see whether it would break?

If marriage is released from its present bonds and humanity redeemed from the vice of hypocrisy, then will adultery gradually be lost sight of, both as a conception and as a deed. Whoever is capable of or feels the desire to commit adultery will simply dissolve the marriage; whoever has occasion to commit adultery has simply found another person with whom he enters into a new marriage. Thus adultery will become a change of marriage, especially when the possibility of finding a person who will serve as a mere tool for an adulterous act can no longer be assumed after women have become independent of men and no longer know what it is to give themselves up to prostitution. For in order to assume the present condition of adultery we must presuppose the present condition of prostitution.

I can foresee that husbands will be frightened at this theory. But I will give them a word of advice. If you wish to keep your wives from adultery, see to it that they can love you ; do not charge it to them as a crime if they love you no longer, and do not force them into hypocrisy if they love some one else. Try to bind them only in so far that they are to tell you openly when another has gained their heart, and then part from them in friendship as is becoming to humane men, in order to let them enter, unhindered, a new relationship which promises them greater happiness. If they can be sure of this humane treatment and this liberty, then you can also generally be sure that they will not deceive you. But the man who wishes to hold the woman in the bonds of marriage, although she no longer loves him, is both a fool and a barbarian, and deserves that badge with which women are wont to distinguish tyrannical husbands.

How much has adultery already been moralized over by priests and disputed over by jurists! And what barbarities has it not called forth! Among almost all savages man has the right to kill the adulterous women without further preliminaries. Among the ancient Egyptians the woman's nose was cut off, because a woman " who incited to forbidden joys had to be deprived of the most

beautiful ornament of a beautiful face." Her
seducer was punished with lashes, yet she was the
" charmer." Among the Hindoos the woman
was publicly torn to pieces by dogs, and the
seducer was fastened upon a red-hot iron bed-
stead and roasted alive. Among the Jews the
adulteress was stoned, but the adulterer was punished only when he had committed the act with a
married woman and had thus (by a violation of
" property") offended another man. According to
the laws of Solon, the Athenian could sell the
adulterous woman as a slave. The Romans permitted the husband to kill both the wife surprised
in the act of adultery and, with her, the adulterer.
Mohammed granted the husband the right to in-
carcerate the sinful woman in an especial apart-
ment of his house " until either death released her
or God gave her a means of escape." Among the
old Teutons the woman, with hair cut off, and dis-
robed, was cast out of the house by her husband
and whipped through the town.

What a list of brutalities and barbarities! And
what for? For an imaginary crime against imaginary masters who called themselves husbands and
were nothing but despots and barbarians.

DIVORCE.

THE laws of a people on divorce are a sure measure of the reasonableness and humanity of its conceptions of marriage.

No nation known to me has reasonable divorce laws. Through the French revolution reason prevailed on this point for a time, in that it made divorce depend on the will of the married couple ; but it soon again succumbed to the old prejudices and narrow-mindedness.

The free, common-sense conception of marriage, and with it also of divorce, is everywhere still suppressed by the theological conception of the relationship between man and woman. So-called religion and the ghostly " God " are the first enemies of marital happiness. According to the theological conception, taking its departure from superhuman consecration and superhuman will, marriage is in itself a hallowed relationship, and this abstract relation in itself, not the real happiness and interest of those who constitute it, is the chief object. Marriage, the formal relationship with the "divine" stamp, is to be upheld even if the married persons perish in it ; marriage is to continue for life, even after all the requirements which constitute its essence have long ago disappeared. Marriage is to make the married persons, not the married persons marriage. Married people exist for the sake of marriage, not marriage for the sake of married people. Though, after becoming acquainted and familiar with each other to a degree not permissible or possible before marriage, they should tire of each other ; though they should hate and loathe each other ; though they should become as disgusting to each other as horrible pictures— they have once been married, they are called husband and wife, they have become a common social firm, they have a " claim " upon each other, they have once for all become *I and you*, and must never again become *I and I*. To be sure, nobody, not even the most bigoted theologian, says that marriage is destined to be an institution of unhappiness, and the marital chamber a chamber of torture ; but if it has come to be so, it must remain so, because otherwise—marriage might become what it ought to be, namely, a relationship based on spontaneous affection, which is formed without help, and, even without force, is not dissolved, just because it finds in this affection, in the satisfaction of the mutual heart interests, the only true, the only legitimate, and the only lasting bond of union.

It is due to the theological, inhuman, misanthropical, barbaric conception of marriage that the laws inflict punishment upon those married persons who no longer respect a relationship

that has become impossible. The " punishment "
visited upon the married couple in their inability
to longer love each other is not sufficient ; for this
very punishment they must be punished. They
have entered into a relationship " for life," it is
said. They may have done so, but they did it
only in the belief that they would be happy with
each other as long as possible, perhaps until
death ; but after they have come to recognize
that they were mistaken ; when, under circumstances which could not have been estimated or
controlled before, they have come to know each
other from a new point of view, which excludes all
happiness and, therefore, the entire object of
marriage, they must, even . when they separate
peacefully and with mutual understanding in order
to seek for happiness elsewhere, be seized by a
theological marriage-police and be chastised for
sinning against the holy marriage relation. This
is the logic of the theological conception.

The duration " for life " is the consequence of
a real marriage, a happy choice ; but to make it
into an obligatory requirement even for an unfortunate choice is to condemn two people to life-
long misery for a momentary weakness, or an innocent chance, or a one-sided guilt, by means of the
most senseless tyranny, simply in order to have
them retain the name of a married couple. Sexual contact or a priestly " blessing " is to deprive
two people completely of their liberty, is to make

of them a mutual galley to which the one has chained the other as his slave, is to be considered as an act *which can never be corrected*. This is certainly logical ; for the infallible stupidity of theology surely cannot be corrected.

Just as it is a truth which must never be lost sight of that progress of society in one direction can never be thought of by itself alone, so it is also impossible to bring about a true married and family life without a general revolution of social ideas and conditions. This does not, however, preclude those, who can in themselves make up for or do without this general revolution from demanding freedom from legal bonds, or from anticipating it ; nor does it preclude the law from even now being shaped with a view to the anticipated conditions of the future. I believe that even on the basis of our present conditions no danger would accrue to society if the law should decree the following :

1) A marriage shall be dissolved when both parties demand a dissolution, and

a) declare that their economical relations are completely settled, which declaration shall absolve them from all future obligations ;

b) documentarily testify that they have agreed about the support and education of their children, which agreement shall be mutually maintained with legal assistance. Legal assistance shall be rendered gratis.

2) A marriage shall be dissolved when one party against the will of the other, has three times, at intervals of one month, demanded a dissolution. In such cases the economical affairs shall be settled legally, if it cannot be done by voluntary agreement. The children shall be awarded to the parents according to their sex, if not otherwise voluntarily agreed. The obligation for the support of the children shall, as a general thing, be placed upon both parties in proportion to the property, if the matter cannot be settled by a free understanding.

By such regulations the character of a compulsory institution might be taken from marriage, and yet every consideration which would have to be taken of present social conditions be allowed for. And the levity which would be inclined to make of marriage a relation of unscrupulous frivolity would be met more effectively by the prospect of the obligations agreed upon than by present laws.

More senseless divorce laws than those of North America cannot easily be found,—doubly senseless for the reason that the forming of marriage is made so easy as to depend on a mere word. A mere promise of marriage, given perhaps in a moment of rashness, of intoxication, etc., can compel marriage ; but the dissolution of the marriage is generally possible only when, after long, expensive, and scandalous lawsuits, the one party has suc-

ceeded in proving against the other the charge of
—adultery. The hope for divorce, therefore, depends solely on scandal.

A New York court, in a suit of this kind,
has just given a decision by which a marriage was
dissolved on account of the proven adultery of
the (seventeen-year-old) wife. The husband was
left free to marry again, " just as if the divorced
wife were dead ;" but the wife was debarred from a
new marriage "until the divorced man had really
died."

A more senseless, more immoral, more unnatural, and more unjust decision I have never heard
of ; but it is only an application of existing laws.

I will not stop to speak of the indirect induce-
ment that such a decision could become to the
condemned party to remove the arbitrary hin-
drance to marriage by criminal means.

Neither will I dwell on the fact that the divorced woman has been condemned by the court
either to an unnatural and not-to-be-expected re-
nunciation, or to permanent prostitution and
shame.

Nor will I discuss the question whether a court
can deny one who has not been found guilty of a
. criminal offence his or her natural or civil rights.

I will not even stop to consider the logic which
• by the divorce destroys every bond, every connection between the divorced parties, and yet restores
this connection by making the woman through

Pages 119-134 missing

RELIGION.

WHAT has been said above of marriage and divorce will be a plain hint to thinking women as to the importance of liberation from the bonds of religious belief. But this point is too important, and the questions attaching to it are too interesting, for me not to devote a separate chapter to it.

It is undeniable that woman is inferior to man in the vigor and logic of her thought as well as of her will. It is, therefore, quite apart from the greater lack of opportunity for intellectual development, generally much harder for her than for man to form for herself an intelligent view of a liberal philosophy which has done away with the teachings of religious belief. On the other hand, woman is emotionally receptive and has an active imagination, and is, therefore, more accessible to the seductive or imposing words of the pious than man. Moreover, her position and her sufferings supply ample need for comfort, which, as is well known, only faith, " the church," is able to give.

Thus it can be explained that it must be more difficult to cure women than men from the religious malady. Weak woman is still everywhere the prey of the priests where men have already shaken off the yoke, and assuredly those black-coated gentlemen would entirely emigrate from many a country if suddenly there were no more women.

But the more difficult it may be for woman to withdraw herself from the influence of the priests and from those teachings which afford the priests their bread and butter, the more necessary this emancipation has become for her. It would lead me too far in this place if I should attempt to revolutionize the religious world of the women by purely rational conceptions of the supernatural and superhuman things by which, in the name of religion, their mind is biassed and intimidated. This has been done on another occasion. (See " Six Letters to a Pious Man.") It must and will become clear to the women that they above all are interested in the recognition of pure humanity, of which they *par excellence* are the most beautiful representatives, but that there can be no thought of this recognition as long as the human being and its happiness is sacrificed to the fictitious objects of a nebulous religious world and despotic authorities. Moreover, the religions, made by men, are all designed to relegate woman to a subordinate position, who, in order to find her lot endurable, must attribute it to a "God." This "God" is nothing more than an invisible overseer of women for the benefit of the men, who hold them as slaves. For a joke, the women ought to give him the companionship of a goddess, whose duty it should be to control him. She might be called Mrs. God.

Let no woman fear to lose her "moral hold" after throwing off the bondage of religion. I have known women who have freed themselves from everything that is known as belief through their own reason, and again others who have been brought up without anything of what is generally called religion. They are more moral, more humane, more wholesome, fresher, and more lovable than all those who have allowed their souls to be adulterated by the morbid views of a religious teaching which is inimical to nature. In the woman the true and the right is already present, crystallized as it were; she only needs to protect herself from harmful influences, she needs only the courage to follow her natural inclinations, and she can be sure that she will not miss her destination and will not go astray on the road of her purely human mission. What often becomes clear to the man only after long reflection, sometimes flashes up in the woman at once. The vigor and logic of thought are in her replaced by more direct and more correct operations of the feelings and a sort of mental sight. But where a female nature has once attained the strength to translate the language of the feelings into the language of thought, she is capable of surprising the most daring philosopher. I call attention to George

Sand, whose ideas on the emancipation of woman and whose psychological expositions of the most beautiful sides of ennobled humanity shame and astonish us men.

There is nothing more pitiable than the fact that the greater part of the sex that preéminently represents beauty and joy pines away in the bondage of disagreeable and joyless powers. As spring beside winter, so does this dark, odious, dehumanized priesthood stand beside the joyous, poetic, humane Grecian world, whose goddess was beauty and whose religion was joy. A second Greece will one day arise, an ennobled Greece, which will expiate the sins of the old by a complete recognition of the feminine sex. *A second, revised edition of Greece* designates the stage towards the attainment of which the entire aspirations of our present development must be directed.

It requires a great deal to take from man in general the religious need (I am not at all speaking of the æsthetic need) to embody his thoughts, desires, hopes, and ideals in pictures, or to worship them in symbols. It is, therefore, possible that the age of complete mental liberty will be bridged over by a period of philosophic-artistic romanticism; by a sort of new mythology which will represent the results of our historical development and of the moral ideals in works of art, and make them the objects of a new cult. If the objects of this cult only are the right ones, then it will beautify life without impeding development. It will especially afford opportunities to draw art into the foreground and lead it towards its destination, which is: the enriching, beautifying, and ennobling of public life. Architecture as well as sculpture, painting as well as music, eloquence as well as poetry, will in the future actually be placed, and that, forsooth, in the sense of the highest end of art, in the service of the collectivity, the State, the people; the craving of men for elevation above the every-day affairs of life will be satisfied through art, and the churches will be changed into temples of art or into theatres. Is it not wonderful that our church-goers, where the want of reason and humanity does not stagger them, are not repulsed at least by the want of poetry and taste? In the simple garden of the Tuileries at Paris, with its statues and promenades. more religion is to be found than in Notre Dame and all the other churches of the metropolis, But what is the garden of the Tuileries in comparison to public resorts which have been purposely created from the desire and the idea to satisfy the ennobled sense of the people for the forms of beauty and the embodiment of thought?

An entirely new world is here opened up to man, and to the statesman who has an eye for more than the things of mere vulgar use. On the other hand, he will be filled with anger and disgust if he must daily be a witness of the way in which the rich means of society are squandered on nonsensical, absurd, and vulgar institutions, while they could so easily be employed for creations which even by their mere external form, would elevate the sense of the people, would ennoble its taste, and give its ideas ethical tone. The mere visit to a beautifully located, tastefully arranged promenade has a more ennobling influence upon the coarsest of men than a visit to the most beautiful church; lingering in a beautifully equipped temple of art does more for the moral nature than all temples of "God;" the construction of a single Greek theatre would be more important for civilization than a thousand institutions of "edification."

Space does not permit me to develop my ideas on this rich theme more minutely. I will only call attention to the fact that the state of civilization, or the capacity for civilization, of a people or a single individual can surely be estimated best according to the degree of their susceptibility to the ideas of the *democratic world of beauty*, an expression by which I mean to comprise everything pertaining to this subject. France, Italy, and Germany are foremost in this respect. In proportion to its means, England is the most backward; and if London did not at least have its Westminster Abbey and its excellent parks, excellent, to be sure, more on account of their size than their arrangement, it would be completely submerged in shopocracy and priest rule. As far as America is concerned, we cannot make any demands without considering the newness of the life here; but even in spite of this consideration, one can easily feel discouraged and repelled by the preponderance of the spirit of ignorance and materialism throughout public life. And yet American development is perhaps not too far removed from the need of the noble man. The influx of European intellect and the headlong speed of the materialistic scramble will perhaps soon create an opposite tendency which will thrive all the better the fewer the impediments the State institutions will put in its way.

Let us, therefore, also hope for a Greek future in America. But as regards the women now, let them, in view of the coming beautiful age of an ennobled Greece, manifest their taste meanwhile in a passive way by learning to do without the confessional and prayers, without nunneries and · calvaries. At the same time, let them improve whatever other opportunities present themselves daily, to the end of removing the priesthood and excluding its influence. I will mention only one thing. The Catholic "Church" regards only those marriages as valid that have received her "blessing;" she does not recognize divorce, and does not permit the remarriage of divorced persons. It is reasonable that a power bent at all hazards on subjugating the spirit should attempt

to make the satisfaction of human needs dependent on its permission or conditions, in order to
become in this way the mistress of the entire man,
and to remind him every moment of his dependence.   The Catholic " Church " has, therefore, also
introduced a great number of fast-days, etc., in
order to rule over man even in the matter of eating and drinking.   And how should she have forgotten to rule over him in the matter of sexual
love!   But she exercises the most exquisite
cruelty of authority by the prohibition which
makes it impossible for divorced people to marry
again.   This prohibition means in other words :
" The more unhappy people feel, the more they
need our consolation ; the more unhappy marriages are, the more occasion have we to intrude
into family life, and especially to take advantage
of the helpless women.   We are the physicians
who make the cure of diseases a crime in order to
secure the longest possible control of the patients.
We must, therefore, seek to prevent the dissolution of marriages ; to that end we refuse to recognize divorce ; and in order to erect another barrier
against the temptation to secure one nevertheless
against our will in a merely legal way, we make it
an impossibility or a crime to marry again for
those who are narrow enough to regard no marriage as valid without the blessing of the priest."

It is in the power of women wherever civil marriage obtains to upset the humane calculation of

the priests. Let them content themselves with civil marriage, and after a possible divorce—do the same thing. No sensible woman ought any longer to consent to the self-degradation of permitting the desecrating hand of a priest to " bless " her love. Shame ! These pestilent propagators of ignorance and disgust ! Every bride must cast a doubt on her taste and her loveliness, if she can consent to let a priest bless, *i.e.*, desecrate, her affection.

I call the attention of women to still another point. I maintain that piety, faith, in brief the occupation with the other world, that is, with a world and with beings that have no existence, is just as pernicious to men's love towards women as the veneration of a ruler makes impossible all true relations among citizens. Whatever a man sends out to an imaginary being beyond the clouds in the shape of feeling, fancy, enthusiasm, " love," he withdraws from the real beings here who exist before his eyes, who associate with him, and to whom he ought to give his whole heart and mind. But if man will take what he has hitherto wasted on the skies back to the earth, into life, into mankind, then first he will become man in reality and learn to make of his fellow-men what they can and ought to be. Woman becomes his "God," and love his " heaven," and mankind his "immortality." Do not smile, ladies, but regard it as in sober earnest when I say to **you** : only the unbeliever is capable of truly loving a woman, and piety exists forever only at the expense of true humanity.

But to return to our Greek ideal. Ancient Greek life was simple, natural ; the Greek life of the future, as the outgrowth of the entire preceding history, will for this reason also prove infinitely more varied, more conscious, and nobler. Womankind also must, therefore, be thought of quite differently from what we see in the figures of Greek women, which are indeed noble and classically simple, but for this very reason also somewhat monotonous and inflexible. Hitherto we have for sought ideals, in the representations of the plastic arts, especially among the ancient Greeks. I am of the opinion that this has been unjust towards a later development, and has too much disregarded the laws of this development. Who doubts that historical life is progressive instead of retrogressive in all directions? And why, even if classic Greece in its specific combination could not repeat itself as a whole, should not individual elements be found in the entire rich field of history which, if a later age should again construct of them a whole, must produce a richer and nobler life than that of the Greeks has been? (We do not even mention here the political anomalies and inhumanities of the Greeks.) It can hardly be contested that we are more advanced than the Greeks, not only in the sciences,

but also in art. But we are not only in advance
of them in the wealth of our world of conceptions,
of knowledge, of ideas, of means, but also in more
beautiful *human ideals.* It is that which is generally overlooked in adhering to our stereotyped
school education and imitation. Not only in
intellectual and spiritual but also in a physical
respect our age can show more beautiful human
beings than the Greek. *The intermingling of the
nations,* from which the Greeks were still very
much excluded, and which, besides, could only
take place very gradually, is a means for the perfection not only of the intellectual but also of the
physical man.

I have had opportunity to make manifold observations among both sexes of the most diverse
nations. The most beautiful women—in order
to speak of these—I have found in America
and England, at least in so far as concerns color
and contour of face. But what is generally
wanting to those finely cast although sometimes
somewhat stereotyped features is the *soul.* They
are, in spite of their purity, too sharp, without
softness, intellectual penetration, plasticity, and
poetry. They look at us, as it were, like cold
crystallizations of beauty, in which there is no active ferment of passion, or of feeling, or of imag
ination ; in short, no deep soul-life. This beautiful
dough of human development is generally desti-
tute of the real yeast of feeling and soul. That

is not only due to the state of culture but, at the
same time, to the national mixture. As far as
form is concerned, the English women, even
when a small French foot might entitle one to
the best conclusions, are frequently deformed by
a most conspicuous breadth of waist. The mixture in America, however much it still betrays
the English type, has already produced much
more perfect forms than in England. The English length of limb, which is so apparent in both
men and women, also has already partly been lost.
In London a lady told me : " The English women
must be admired on the balcony, the French on
the street." She was not enough of a physiolo-
gist to make clear the truth of her assertion by
describing the forms. The American women
seem to have acquired some French attributes ;
perhaps they are only wanting some German ones
in order to complete the transition of the feminine world into a new Greek era.

I believe that ideals of beauty cannot very well be native to
those nations which bear too much of a national
stamp in their external appearance. The ideal
body as well as the ideal mind must be cosmopol-
itan, and they are to be found in Germany and
France.

I believe that according to character as well as
physique the French and the Germans, *i.e.*, French
men and German women, or German men and
French women, are above all destined to estab-

lish by intermingling the new generation of a nobler race on European soil. French spirit and German character, German intellect and French vivacity ; French fire and German strength, German feeling and French grace ; French sense and German sentiment, German thoughts and French impulses ;—those are the elements whose union would necessarily constitute the ideal of true humanity, and would correspond with each other as the blue-eyed and the brown-eyed races correspond physically.

The intermingling of the nations is so important a condition of development that without it we may expect actual stagnation. In those peoples which are most completely shut off from the intercourse of the nations civilization is stagnant like a swamp, and only the lower spheres of development are active. One need only call to mind China, Spain, partly also insular England, especially Ireland. Italy as well as Greece for a long time seemed to be doomed to a similar fate. Perhaps the Austrian admixture was destined to revivify the noble Italian blood to such an extent that it was able to pour itself in new fermentation into the stream of human development, and thus subjugation had also in this respect to become a means of progress. It seems, moreover, that the mixture-ferments, which start the development of a people, as for instance in Italy and Greece, outlive themselves after a certain time, or lose their vital force, and that then a resuscitation must first take place before development can thrive anew. I shall not enlarge upon these suggestions. They lead to one of the most interesting speculations concerning the development of many-sided humanity.

I recommend it in passing to the earnest consideration of our artists who cannot yet break loose from the old-fogyism of the schools, which leads them again and again to make their studies, instead of among living men, only among dead statues,—instead of in the moving present, only in immobile antiquity. Two thousand years after Christ they will find quite different human ideals than two hundred years before the crucifixion.

But the women, I hope, will not resent it if I also direct their attention to the meeting and intermingling of the nations, which is the quietly effective means for the universal ennobling of humanity, but which can take place only in a condition of complete liberty where every obstacle of mutual prejudice, mutual embarrassment, and mutual egotism will be torn down. The graces of the arts and the genii of humanity can only take up their abode where a free spirit in free intercourse has domesticated the best and the most beautiful which human development has produced in the course of the centuries.

But the philistines will ask why this chapter bears the heading " Religion,"

THE ECONOMIC INDEPENDENCE OF WOMAN.

IF we are to speak of freedom, and especially of free marriage, we must above all things establish the independence of the individual, and especially the mutual independence of husband and wife.

The great question of the times, to secure an existence to every one and thus to protect him, on the one side, from material want and, on the other side, to liberate him from conditions in which material dependence makes him a mere tool of others—this great question concerns no one more closely than the women. Let it but be borne in mind what has been said above of prostitution. Perhaps seven-eighths of the feminine sex are dependent, or degraded, or enslaved, or prostituted because—they cannot emancipate themselves economically from the men.

If the solution of the problem of existence, so far as it concerns the male sex, is already difficult enough, in the interests of the women it is still more difficult to solve. The practical course of events brings it about that the men, since they are the makers of history, want their turn to come first and make it come first; moreover, the men are equipped for the work of life, while the women have hitherto had to attach their existence chiefly to that of the men, and are in general not brought up in a way to be able at once to stand on their own feet. Most women, therefore, are still in want of one more requisite than the men, namely, the education for work.

But let us make it clear to ourselves that one step in progress always presupposes another. If we, therefore, have to recognize the inability of most women under the present circumstances to gain for themselves an independent existence, it does not follow from this that the same conditions will hold for the future. Let us make this clear by laying down several points.

1) The State of the future secures to women as well as to men, free of charge, an all-sided opportunity for the development of their native abilities.

2) Education in the future will be considerably facilitated and more equalized between the two sexes, since the sciences become ever more simplified, popularized, and their results made more accessible to every one, while at present their secrets are still hidden behind the learned barricades of the scholars' caste. In the future many a lay person will know more than many a professor knows now, for the chaff of unnecessary knowledge will be winnowed away, and true knowledge will reduce everything to the pure kernel. If we consider hereby that women have the same or greater abil-

ity than men for the learning and executing of a
thousand things, but have hitherto only been kept
from them by education, we must imagine their
circle of activity in the future to be much greater
than it has so far been.

3) In a more humane development of the State
ever more positions will be opened up in which
only the *woman* will find a place, while in the
present state of public affairs men are employed
almost exclusively. Let us only think of the future
schools of all sorts, the institutions of art, of
amusement, the workhouses, hospitals, the institutions for the reception of the "*enfants de la
patrie*" (as they very beautifully call the foundlings in Paris), the institutions for the reformation
of prostitutes, etc., and we shall find a thousand
opportunities not only for the maintenance but for
the noble occupation of women of which no one
has so far thought.

4) The State will continually gain more means
to secure beforehand the satisfaction of the prin-
cipal needs of its citizens through public institutions, and thus to facilitate or to simplify the
individual's care for his existence, and therefore
will be able to furnish not only the entire public
education free of cost, but also the public amuse-
ments and perhaps even the dwellings (at least for
those without means). State help will be extended all the more to women, especially the more the
principle comes to be recognized that the disabled

must be maintained by the collectivity, and that those without work must be furnished with adequate occupation by the State.

These are some of the suppositions from which we must reason in order to judge the future economic position of women ; and if one considers that the woman requires much less for her maintenance than the man, a great part of the difficulty of self-support will be equalized by her fewer wants.

But let this difficulty, to enable the woman to establish an independent existence, be ever so great, it suffices that, as a human being and as a member of the body social, she has the same right to such an existence as the man. The ways and means to solve this problem of existence the State of the future will no doubt find when it has created those liberties and those truly democratic institutions which permit all legitimate interests to assert themselves, and allow of the unhindered disposition of public means. But when that problem is once solved, woman will gain quite a different esteem and position. She will no longer be forced to sell her body as a tool for lust ; she will no longer be under the necessity of accepting the next best opportunity to get married, but will be able to make her choice according to her true inclination ; there will be greater opportunity for this than hitherto, for now the impossibility to maintain a family excludes many a man from marriage who could otherwise make a woman happy (the standing armies alone, which are to be abolished in the future, condemn thousands to a single life and to prostitution who would in a rational State become useful members of society and good husbands); she will be able to maintain her independence in marriage, and will not submit to unworthy treatment from fear of being without the means of subsistence after a dissolution of the relationship; she will, in one word, be able as a human being to secure her liberty, as a citizen her right, as a wife her dignity, and as a woman her happiness.

But the economic independence of woman, as well as her ethical appreciation, can only be attained after the bad conditions of the present are completely changed, and the edifice of the true state has been erected on the ruins of these bad conditions. Therefore the women must join the great public conspiracy, which, where reform is sufficient, will strive to better the condition of humanity by reform and, where revolution is necessary, by revolution. And since a just regulation of the economic conditions is thinkable only through a true democracy in which the majority of the suffering can take their interests into their own hands, woman's interests from the start assign her a place in the truly democratic party; and since the true democracy will hardly be established anywhere without revolutionary attacks on power and money, woman is from the start assigned to the revolutionary party.

LIBERTY AND THE REVOLUTION THE ALLIES OF WOMEN.

IN the same degree that the true liberty of men is great and well developed the position of women naturally becomes freer and more favorable. Now even if her legal position is as yet nowhere equal to that of the male sex, because complete liberty has as yet nowhere become a reality, it still is important to recognize by illustrations the differences in the shaping of the destinies of women as the results of the greater or lesser liberties of a people.

Let us for this purpose contrast North America with monarchical countries. In the greater part of Europe the legal enactments which determine the legal position of women are sometimes the outcome of manifest barbarity. The Code Napoléon, for instance, surrenders women entirely to the lusts of men by prohibiting the establishment of the paternity of an illegitimate child.* But the man has full power over the woman, as he can compel her with the help of the police to remain in his house, while the opposite is not the case.

---

* Code Napoléon, art. 340: La recherche de la paternité est interdite.—TRANSLATOR.

The man is the master and guardian over the wife and her children. The Prussian government, forced by the fruits of its military system, stands by illegimate children in so far as to permit suits for alimony, etc.; but to make up for this it grants the husband the right by means of "mild chastisement" to remind his wife of the fact that she is at bottom nothing but his slave.

In North America we have at least overcome such ideas of right; and even if the rights of woman are neither completely recognized nor guarded here, the *consciousness of the wrong* that is being done them, and the endeavor to do them justice, find expression in social life as well as in law.

The attention which the Americans show to the women in social intercourse is known the world over. But far be it from me to take it for anything else than a sort of conventional sin-offering for rights withheld. It is for the most part mere gallantry. But there are no more dangerous "virtues" than piety and gallantry. Behind the first, rascality is wont to hide itself; behind the latter, coarseness. Gallantry is nothing more than a cheap substitute for true appreciation, the justice of which is felt more than admitted; it is a deceptive humility with which one deceives himself and others concerning the arrogance that is hidden behind it. But since it springs just as much from a vague perception as from conscious arrogance, it is at once a proof of the necessity or the inclination to grant to women what belongs to them.

The consciousness of the wrong due towards women is moreover expressed in American legislation. It is indeed much that the men have conceded to women the right to put them out of conceit with their own want of principle by allowing the women to claim a mere promise of marriage as a binding contract. But, on the other hand, this legal precaution shows that the least conception of the true essence of marriage is wanting, for a relationship which is brought about only through the intervention of the police is no marriage from the start, but an institution of force which can only breed disaster. And such regulations generally accrue only to the benefit of unworthy women who either disclaim all feeling of self-respect and honor to such a degree that they will allow a man to be bound to them by force who is not drawn to them by any inclination, or who are low enough to actually speculate on promises of marriage in order to get themselves provided for. Whether, moreover, the right to establish a promise of marriage by a mere oath is not most dangerous in a moral respect is a question which experience is not slow to answer.*

---

* The following interesting case of perjury is said to have happened in Philadelphia several years ago. A handsome young man is summoned before the judge to give an explanation of himself concerning a promise of marriage. He does not remem-

"Liberty and equality" must not only be realized with regard to *classes*, but also with regard to the *sexes*. From this we are still far removed, even in America. Especially the marriage and divorce laws, as we have seen above, are still sufficiently barbaric here. The above-mentioned symptoms, however, coupled with isolated regulations, which partly emancipate the women from the economic control of the men, as well as isolated attempts to increase this emancipation through legislation, plainly show how great a start the liberty of American women has already secured, as com-

---

ber ever having made such a promise. But the judge sets aside all doubts by the assurance on oath of a beautiful lady with whom the young man after various denials is finally confronted. He had never seen the lady. But she insists that he, on the occasion of a secret rendezvous, has promised to marry her, and claims him for a husband. The astonished candidate for marriage assures her that her beauty and amiability gave the best proof to the contrary, for force was not needed to make him the husband of a woman who was fitted to meet all his requirements, and for this reason she would certainly believe him if he insisted that he had never seen her before. The lady, however, adheres to her oath, and the marriage is concluded at once. On the way home the young wife confesses to her husband that his appearance had long ago excited her love, but as she found no opportunity to make his acquaintance, she at last struck upon the desperate expedient of seeking it by means of perjury. Now after having attained her end she gave him back his full liberty and would, in case he should want a divorce, agree to it at once. The divorce, however, was not sought.

pared with that of European women, in a legal
respect.

But their chief advantage consists in the liberty
to agitate, and in that freedom from prejudice
which allows them to themselves take an active
part in the work of emancipation, as the woman
conventions have shown.

But with this liberty they have not yet accomplished enough.   True liberty does not appear like
an oasis in the desert of barbarity surrounding it.
Liberty, wherever it appears, stands in the closest
connection, in constant interchange, with all other
branches of development and with all mundane
conditions.   There is no narrower prejudice than
that which considers American development independent of European development, which is its
mother.   That does not only concern politicians,
but also women.   I do not speak of the fact that
American women can gain an infinitely greater
store of conceptions from the literature of Germany and France, from the profound discussions
of the social and humane questions in Europe,
than from the limited literature of materialistic
America.   But I should especially like to make it
clear to them that it is indirectly for their greatest
interest to see the ideas which have been awakened
through German and French literature translated
to action and life by the victory of the European
revolution.   The victory of the European revolution over barbarity and darkness will also have an

immense influence upon North America. If the air has been cleared by a thunder-shower over there, many a cloud will likewise disappear in the West from the heaven of humanity. The world has not yet been turned around, and now as before the sun will rise in the East, even if the revolution of our earthly sphere begins from the West.

As I have shown in a former article, wholesale murder, the warrior's trade, constitutes the chief advantage upon which the male sex, consciously or unconsciously, founds its chief prerogative as against the feminine sex. What now will be the chief result of the victory of the European revolution? The interest which American women have in this victory can be made clear in a short series of conclusions.

What directly establishes the predominance of men and their inhuman tyranny over women? As we have seen, *war*, wholesale murder.

Who causes the wars with all their consequences of bestiality, and in whose favor are they waged? In favor of monarchs!

What enables monarchs to wage these wars, and what continually dulls the judgment in regard to the outrage of the " glorious " trade of murder? The standing armies!

How can monarchs, wars, and standing armies be abolished in Europe? By establishing republics!

What will be the universal consequence of Europe republicanized? Peaceful union of the nations and mutual disarmament!

What follows from all this? *The great interest which American women have in the establishment of the European republic!*

Thus the republicanization of Europe is an affair whose result must have revolutionizing influence on the conditions and the development of the whole world, especially of America. Will America have to remain prepared for war when the main portion of the world is republicanized, the nations are fraternized, and their destiny taken out of the hands of the barbarous god of war and placed in the hands of a peaceful congress of nations? Will playing soldiers, which for the men of this republic seems to have become the only poetry of national life, still have any reason for being? When this military diversion for the national mind shall have ceased, will not nobler conceptions and needs force themselves to the surface? Is not militarism the prop of everything unfree, and the foil for every vulgarity? But vulgarity is the greatest evil of North America. This vulgarity also makes all true national life and national festivity impossible, whereby women lose every opportunity of making their influence felt in public social intercourse, and of making themselves appreciated.

These suggestions will suffice for far-seeing women to justify me in positively declaring that the European revolution is the most powerful ally of the women of America as well as of Europe.

CONCLUSION.

WOMEN in general still make themselves the slaves of fashion ; their heart is set on gewgaws, and they grow enthusiastic over a thousand trifles. To please women in general one must be a man without intellect or heart. Women in general— but why talk of all these things ?   I pass them by all the more readily because they stand in relation with most of the chief evils examined above. This examination, the critical and reformatory survey of the existing chief evils, their causes, their relation, and the means of abolishing them, was the only thing of importance.

The fair readers must have become convinced by this survey that their oppression, their dependence, their degradation is founded on

the rule of force,

the rule of money, and

the rule of priests.

It must, therefore, have become clear to them that they cannot depend on an improvement of their lot before

the liberty and the right of all men have been attained,

the existence of all men has been secured, and

the essence and dignity of all men have been recognized in purely human conceptions.

Everything that they can be and can wish for depends on these three points: their liberty, their rights, their dignity, their social position, their marital happiness, their love, their education, their everything.

Therefore these three points also suffice as a guide to women for the direction which their antipathies and sympathies, their hate and their love must take. Let all despotism with its supporters, all aristocracy of wealth with its representatives, all religious humbug with its priests, be recommended to the hatred and the abhorrence of the women; let liberty with its champions, socialism with its apostles, reason with its teachers, appeal to the love and sympathy of all women of right thought and noble feeling, whose striving, whose interests, whose happiness, whose future do indeed lie only in the path of these revolutionary motors.

Let them but smile upon you, entice you, flatter you, those brilliant despots, those perfumed slave-holders, those gay soldiers, those suave diplomatists, those proud money-lords, those fawning priests—turn your backs on them, cast them from you with contempt, and swear to them the hatred of destruction, for they are the creators of your slavery, the fathers of your shame, the teachers of your degradation. Only free men are your

friends, and only with the era of complete liberty
and justice does the morning of your true being
dawn for you.

Powerless and degraded as you have hitherto
been, you can attain to power and distinction
from the moment that you combine with the correct appreciation of your ends the sincere will to
serve them. Your tender hands are a thousand-
fold able to interfere in the course of events and
the actions of men, if you will only put them in
the service of your hatred and your love, and if
you will hate what is bad and love what is right.
You can encourage and deter; you can reward
and you can punish; you can twine wreaths
and crowns of thorns. If a virgin, cast off your
suitor if he does not prove himself a servant
of liberty. If a wife, desert your husband if
he deserts the cause of liberty. If a mother,
rear your children on the milk of liberty, and
early enflame in their hearts the hatred for
tyranny, that the dagger of Harmodious and
Aristogeiton may become the plaything of their
youth.

Look about you in Europe! It lies down-
trodden beneath the feet of those in whose eyes
your entire sex is nothing but a herd of servants
and whores, under the feet of those who have had
you flogged beneath the gallows on which they
had hanged your husbands and sons. What will

your future be if in the impending struggles these men again remain the victors?

Look about you in America! It was approaching a time which was to put the stamp of slavery on this entire republic in the name of "democracy." And what would your future have been if this slaveholder democracy had not been overthrown? The poison of corruption would have corroded *all* moral conceptions, and the passion of vulgarity have severed *all* moral ties; expoliation would have completed the right of the stronger, and degradation would have completed the law of the weaker; power would have been taught to rule everything, and money to buy everything; the recognition of the rights of man would have become a stupidity, and the assertion of humanity treason; the standard of the slaveholder would have measured every interest, and the interest that would have been felt for you would have been nothing more than that felt for the women in Europe.

Well, slavery has been abolished, but its chief supports, vulgarity, wealth, the priesthood, have come into the inheritance, and they will endeavor to keep you in a state of semi-slavery until you help to make them harmless by championing science, justice, and enlightenment.

Must you still be told what you are to love and what you are to hate, in America as well as in Europe?

The reaction everywhere reveals three points : force, money rule, priesthood. The points of the opposition are : liberty, justice, reason. The points of the reaction are always the proper targets for the hatred, the points of the opposition always the proper objects for the sympathy, of women. For they, as the weaker party, are always the ones whom the victory of the reaction, continuing to operate, affects most disastrously, and, as the most disqualified party, they are always the ones who receive the greatest aid for their interests in the most radical opposition.

In Europe it is the banner of the revolution, in America the banner of radical democracy, which leads the hosts on towards the time when the free woman can proudly rejoice by the side of the free man. On the grave of the tyrants blooms your liberty, from the ruins of aristocracy arise your rights. Therefore follow the banner of the revolution in Europe, and the banner of radical democracy in America!

It is not for us alone; no, it is for you yourselves, ye women, if you heed the call of the time which says to you :

Women must enter the ranks of the revolution for the object is the *revolution of humanity.*

POSTSCRIPT.

IN a footnote to my preface, the translator of the foregoing treatise has clearly defined her views regarding the means to be employed in the attainment of the *common aim*, and which she considers as radically divergent from those of the author, without, however, in my opinion, at the same time stating the position of her opponent just as clearly. For this reason, as well as in the interest of a better understanding of the matter under discussion, I take occasion to set forth clearly, by means of a succinct *résumé*, Heinzen's views with regard to the important factors in the development of mankind touched upon by the point at issue. It seems to me it will be seen that there are more points of contact in regard to the subject treated therein between the esteemed translator and the author of this treatise, and that at bottom she does not entertain such fundamentally divergent views from his as she feels bound to assume. Heinzen defines the conception of the " State " succinctly as follows :

" ' Democracy.' I supply this term with quotation-marks to indicate that I merely borrow it. For at bottom it does not mean what in the radical sense it ought to mean. Democracy (popular *rule*) is by no means an expression for a rational or appropriate conception. Where there is authority, there must also be servants. But a free people know neither the one nor the other. Over whom are the people to rule? Even their office-holders and agents they can only entrust and commission with their affairs. The term democracy came into use simply to denote an opposition to an authority *over* the people. The people are not to be ruled by others, from which it does not follow, however, that now the people themselves are to establish an authority, but that all authority must disappear. And with the conception of authority the conception of *government* will vanish. All that remains and all that is necessary is a common *administration* according to general vote, a supervision of the common interests conducted by the requisite *personnel* under general control. Control is not authority.

" Of an individual freely attending to his affairs or promoting his interests we say neither that he governs nor that he is governed. Just as little can we say so of a society of individuals who form a voluntary association for a common purpose and call this association a State. And if for the practical attainment of their purpose they entrust or commission certain persons with certain functions, the exercise of these functions will as little constitute an authority or a government as the control of a joint-stock company or any other joint enterprise by a board of experts and trustees. The conception of authority ought, therefore, to be entirely excluded from radical political thought, and with it the term denoting it. The term republic comes much nearer to expressing the nature of a free State than the term democracy. The most proper term perhaps would be, the *commonwealth* (Gemeinwesen). The popular conception of the State is still tainted by the dominating influence of the examples of the past, the historical models, and therefore most men cannot conceive of even the freest State without a dualism of the people and a special power which is called authority and government. Only by a thorough analysis of the conceptions authority and government do we reach a correct understanding of what is meant to be expressed by the term 'democracy,' but what it does not express.

"It is surely not necessary to parry the objection that this definition of the State will lead to what in its bad or good sense is called Anarchy. Anarchy in its bad sense is barbarism, and in its good sense an impossibility. State and Anarchy are contradictions, for a State is as little conceivable *without* as Anarchy *with* organization.

"But organization in the free State is nothing more than order and arrangement of business. I should therefore define it thus : The State is, on a common ground, an association of free and, before

the law, equal individuals for the object of facili-
tating and securing the realization of the life purposes of each individual through the proper au-
thorized agents by means of their jointly created
and supervised institutions, laws, and resources.

" Such a definition of the State—and it is the
only correct one—at once directs each to the
claims that he has to make, but, at the same time,
to the task that he has to perform.   It makes of
him as it were a State business partner, but it also
makes the degree of the satisfaction of his claims
dependent on his direct and indirect participation
in the administration of the business.

" North America is regarded as a 'democratic'
State, and the people in general have learned to
put faith in this term.   The true significance of
this term must become plain to them if, in the con-
templation of existing conditions and their power
of influencing them, they will take the above definition for a standard.   It will appear that we have
indeed an authority here, but an authority *over the
people*—a relation that is not improved, but only
made worse, by the fact that the people themselves
elect their ruler and are thus under the illusion that
they govern.   Whoever has made this clear to himself, and surveys the chasm existing between the
truly free State, as it has been defined above, and
the State we actually have here, he alone will be
able to correctly estimate the consequences of
the repeated endeavors to still farther extend

this authority, and appreciate the necessity of meeting them by the timely spread of radical conceptions of the State.

" It having already been sufficiently discussed in the pamphlet ' What is True Democracy ?', I refrain in this place from any further exposition of the fundamentally anti-democratic representative system, according to which the people surrender themselves powerlessly into the hands of executive as well as legislative representatives who are both irresponsible and, during their term of office, inaccessible. The essential requirement of a free people, on which all others depend, is universal suffrage, and this primary right is partly wanting entirely, and partly threatened where it exists.

"All reasons which are brought forward to justify departures from universal suffrage are only sham reasons. Not only the considerations of human rights, but even the considerations of expediency, admit of absolutely no exception. Logically conceived and carried out, exclusion from suffrage would have to mean exclusion from the State as well. A person without suffrage is an alien, while citizen and voter must be identical. Where the principle of equal rights is once departed from, there no longer any limit is to be drawn for disenfranchisement. If *capacity* is to decide, where then is incapacity to end ? And who is to judge of capacity ? But if even *property* is to be taken as a standard, is not the possessor thus by a two-

fold preponderance made completely the master
of the dependent poor? There is no more monstrous arrogance than to grant to property over
and above the advantages it already confers also
the privilege of authority, a privilege to which, if
it were ever justifiable, only the deepest insight
and the most disinterested concern for the general welfare could grant a claim.

" The dangers which are predicted by the oppo-
nents of equal rights are only imaginary, and in the
course of time will disappear of themselves. The
power of incapacity decreases with increased opportunity to test itself ; and where, as a result of
former neglect, it causes the State temporary em-
barrassments, the latter has to overcome them by a
proper expiation of its own guilt. The State is as
little exempt as the individual from the necessity
of either atoning for former mistakes by righting
them, or of multiplying them to work its own ruin.
The negro slaves had placed this country before
such an alternative, and it decided itself for the
saving expedient in the eleventh hour. After
justice had been done to the negroes, at least as
far as form is concerned, the women knocked at
the doors of the Capitol. We too, they say, are
human beings and are called citizens : we too are
a part of the people, and not its worst part; we
too want to have a part in the associated business
which is called State. You speak of democracy
and exclude one half of society from it, in order

that you as privileged class and usurpers of the State may rule over them. Even if you had abolished all other forms of authority, that of sex, the most senseless of all, you still allow to stand. Do you fear, perchance, that by granting us equal rights you will reap the fruits of the education which you have given us? Very well; it is in your power to give us a different one. Or do you fear that we would destroy the ruinous fruits of your own education? Very well; then allow them to increase until they have ruined you. No other outlet will lead to your as well as to our welfare than justice, and the sooner you will practise it the better it will be both for you and for us. If you do not wish to take upon yourself the risk of the transition, then take upon yourself the risk of destruction.

"Upon due consideration all the evils and dangers which are ascribed to the realization of the equal rights of man in the State are only temporary and fancied. In any case this realization is a categorical imperative of evolution, which can be silenced only by an honest recognition, and the inauguration and preservation of universal suffrage is its first guarantee. There are thousands who possess this right and do not exercise it. Whatever the reason for this neglect may be, let him who has never voted hasten to the polls at least when the issue is to preserve the suffrage for those who already possess it, or to secure it for those who still want it." K. S.

Schriften

von

KARL HEINZEN.

Gedichte. Dritte vermehrte Auflage. (Gesammelte Schriften, erster Band.)

Lustspiele. (Gesammelte Schriften, zweiter Band.)

Erlebtes. Erster Theil. (Gesammelte Schriften, dritter Band.)

Erlebtes. Zweiter Theil. (Gesammelte Schriften, vierter Band.)

Der Editoren-Kongress zu Cincinnati, oder das gebrochene Herz. (Gesammelte Schriften, fünfter Band.)

Teutscher Radicalismus in Amerika. (Gesammelte Vorträge.)

Erster Band (vollständig vergriffen).
Zweiter Band, brochirt, . . $0.75
Dritter Band, gebunden, . 1.00
Vierter Band, gebunden, . 1.00

ESSAYS BY KARL HEINZEN

TRANSLATED INTO ENGLISH:

Communism and Socialism, . . . $0.10
Six Letters to a Pious Man, . . .15
Lessons of a Century, ...10
Separation of State and Church, . . .10
What is Real Democracy? 10
What is Humanity? 10
The True Character of Humboldt, . .10
Murder and Liberty, ...10